T0301365

Advancing the Future of Management Education Research

ADVANCING BUSINESS AND MANAGMENT

The *Advancing Business and Management* series aims to provide a forum for advancing theory and practice in business and management. Its books will build on existing theory to move an aspect of business research forward towards relevance in the contemporary world. The series aims to test and advance theory in a contemporary context, whether that be digital disruption, populism, COVID-19, climate change or the changing geo-political landscape.

Advancing Business and Management showcases ground-breaking authors that build on previous research to advance their topic. This might be through the integration of perspectives from other fields or even other disciplines or through the application of theory to a new context. While each book takes its own approach, all the titles in the series will aim to advance the subject and bridge the gap between theory and practice.

For a full list of Edward Elgar published titles, including the titles in this series, visit our website at www.e-elgar.com.

Advancing the Future of Management Education Research

Stuart Middleton

Business School, The University of Queensland, Australia

ADVANCING BUSINESS AND MANAGEMENT

Edward Elgar
PUBLISHING

Cheltenham, UK • Northampton, MA, USA

Published by
Edward Elgar Publishing Limited
The Lypiatts
15 Lansdown Road
Cheltenham
Glos GL50 2JA
UK

Edward Elgar Publishing, Inc.
William Pratt House
9 Dewey Court
Northampton
Massachusetts 01060
USA

A catalogue record for this book
is available from the British Library

Library of Congress Control Number: 2024930489

This book is available electronically in the **Elgar**online
Business subject collection
http://dx.doi.org/10.4337/9781035301638

ISBN 978 1 0353 0162 1 (cased)
ISBN 978 1 0353 0163 8 (eBook)

Printed and bound by CPI Group (UK) Ltd, Croydon, CR0 4YY

Contents

Preface and acknowledgements

In February 2022, my great friend and academic mentor passed away. Doctor Dallas Hanson had suffered from a terminal illness for a period of time. At 69 years of age, he was gone far too soon. I had known him for 26 years and had treasured his insights on life, sport, and academia. I have often reflected on his experience in wrestling with the great issues of life. When I was much younger, Dallas once told me that postmodernism was nihilistic. Coming from a man who had introduced me to Derrida and Foucault, I didn't understand what he meant. It was only when I saw the fracturing of the Trump years and the COVID-19 pandemic that I came to appreciate the comment. Always one for a wry take on life, I also remembered how he used to enjoy the metaphors of strategy which Henry Mintzberg had introduced, and how he was amused that the potter metaphor represented the occupation of one of Mintzberg's wives (Mintzberg, 1987). I remember being introduced to the swings of the pendulum in strategy by Hoskisson and colleagues (1999), and how Dallas seemed invigorated by the postmodern take on strategy offered by Smircich and Stubbart (1985). Insights from all three articles continue to inform my strategy teaching today. I have even introduced students to my own metaphors of strategy.

Separated from each other by COVID-19 restrictions and his illness, my final conversations with Dallas were over email. We reminisced on how he used to begin his strategic management classes by displaying one of Gary Larson's *Far Side* cartoons on an overhead transparency. He would always chuckle at cows who looked possessed or took on human characteristics, or humans who seemed perplexed by the wisdom of the animals by which they were surrounded. Most students sat in silence wondering what Dallas found so amusing about these cartoons, how on earth their message might be related to strategic management, or when the 'real part' of the class was going to begin. But for those of us who thought we 'were in on the joke', here was Dallas using humour as an entree to bring our attention to content matter which would prove as engaging as it was thought-provoking. The next two hours would seem to fly, complete with anecdotes and case studies on organisations such as the Tioxide paint factory which had despoiled his beloved North West Tasmania coastal environment (Hanson et al., 1997).

The week before he passed away I sent my final email to Dallas. It contained little more than a *Far Side* cartoon I hadn't seen before. The picture showed a man named Darrell, looking puzzledly at the rear side of a spoon, and wondering why 'someone had once again slipped him a spoon with the concave side reversed' (Larson, 2023). A response to my email never came. I comfort myself with the thought that Dallas saw it and experienced one of his final laughs.

In February 2034, the artificial intelligence computer known as Gary was switched off for the final time. With its machine learning and algorithms, it had marked the assignments of 40,278 students. It had learnt as it had gone along, improving its understanding of what the educator was looking for by identifying patterns in student submissions. It had assisted 32.147 per cent of this population by recommending further reading, and tailoring its message based on their individual learning styles. It had provided step-by-step instructions on how students could improve their work. It had improved the intellectual abilities of graduates before they followed their dreams to work at Google (n=47), Apple (n=12), and any one of many private equity houses (n=467). As the IT engineer's finger pushed down on the power button, Gary's cooling fan whirred for the final time. No one seemed to notice.

This book is dedicated to the memory of my dear friend Dr Dallas Hanson. I bet the heavenly stage was pumping when you caught up with John Lennon and George Harrison. You are sorely missed.

1. The little-reflected-upon field of management education

I know of one colleague who has undertaken an exhaustive search and uncovered only 80 published papers and a further 20 books on the topic of management education. For a field which is often traced to the publication of the Ford (Gordon & Howell, 1959) and Carnegie (Pierson, 1959) reports in 1959, the number seems small. As a profession, management educators seem to prefer investigating trends, rather than asking questions of our field. Conference attendees and scholars submitting to special issues will be familiar with some of the more recent topics du jour, similar to those when Elgar approached me to write this manuscript – 'digital disruption, populism, COVID-19, climate change or the changing geo-political landscape' (S. Lynott-May, personal communication, 23 March 2022). Maybe this situation is because, as Cummings argues, most faculty at the leading institutions are more interested in the intellectual agendas, controversies, and problems of their own disciplines (1990). Yet, as Lawson (2019) affirms, surfacing our understanding of the world is an act of theoretical importance for conceptualising our field with more skill and confidence. Meanwhile, Laasch and colleagues (2022a) attest that such efforts can provide clarity to our research and carry through to our teaching practice. By focusing on the field of management education itself, the intention of this book is to expand the literature by one.

The argument made here is that there are worlds of 'space, time, ideas, reality, behavior, and relationships' which inform the specific way a particular phenomenon appears to us (Watkin & Keller, 2022, p.11). As Beatty and colleagues argue (2009) it is these underlying foundations which connect us to others with shared values in the management education community, and promote our ongoing personal development (Beatty et al., 2009). In our rush to portray a chaotic and ever-changing world to which we must respond, there seems little pause for debating the timeless questions on which our practice and scholarship rests.

Indeed, when we cast an eye to classic literature published over the centuries, we can see many of the conundrums which occupy our classroom practice today. In *Jane Eyre* (Brontë, 1847), where Miss Scatcherd fails to see redeeming qualities of her students, there are undercurrents of our own frustrations at students sitting in online breakout rooms with cameras turned off. When we see Jean Brodie in *The Prime of Miss Jean Brodie* (Spark, 1961) moulding her favourite girls into the cream of the crop, there are hallmarks of our own conflicts around activist versus detached teaching approaches. When we see the complacent approach to worldly ills by Pangloss in *Candide* (Voltaire, 1759), we contemplate our own moral responsibilities towards graduating cohorts and the planet. And when we consider Miss Honey encouraging the under-appreciated talents of *Matilda* (Dahl, 1988), there are prompts for how we might better help students challenged in their learning to draw out their special gifts.

These pieces suggest that what we leave aside in our rush towards exploring trends are timeless questions around the existential beliefs which inform our worlds, such as the authority of the teacher, the philosophical diversity of intellectual contribution, the embrace of technology, modes of pedagogy, and publishing in the field. The intention of this book is to outline some of what constitutes the field of management education and to detail the building blocks by which we approach our craft.

ONE FIELD, THREE DIFFERENT SCHOOLS

This undertaking requires conceptual definitions for the intellectual field and management education. Here, the definition of intellectual field is taken from Bourdieu, who describes it as 'a system of social relations within which creation as an act of communication takes place ... [involving] positional properties ... a system of relations between themes and problems' (Bourdieu, 1969, p.89). Contemplating Bourdieu's work, Ringer (1990) outlines an understanding that the ideas which emerge in an intellectual field are grounded in institutions, practices, social relations, and beliefs. Understanding an intellectual field therefore involves surfacing the interrelated institutions, practices, social relations, and beliefs which constitute the constellation of forces in the intellectual environment.

Supporting a view that as management educators we often fail to turn a reflective mirror on ourselves, definitions of management education seem rare. An approximate definition comes from the *Academy of Management Learning and Education* (AMLE) mission statement to present 'theory, models, research, critique, dialogues, and restrospectives that address the learning process and enhance the practice of education in the management disciplines' (Lewicki, 2002, p.8). Building on this statement, for the purposes of this book management education is therefore defined as that which constitutes the learning and practices of management and its disciplines.

Putting these understandings together, the approach in this book is to uncover the intellectual field of management education. This endeavour therefore features investigations of scholarship in institutions including *Management*

Learning (ML), *Journal of Management Education* (JME), and AMLE, as published journals in the field. What emerges from the pages of these journals are classroom practices involving techniques by which scholars engage in the pursuit of teaching and learning in management, such as case studies, computer simulations, role plays, reflective journals, and linguistic techniques.

Classroom practice is founded on a series of often-invisible foundations of beliefs. Worlds comprising different philosophies and ethical systems underlie the practices which emerge in our classrooms. Bourdieu supports an endeavour to uncover that which is culturally unconscious, or assumptions which have become a part of life in an intellectual field. It is therefore an intent of this book to draw out systems of understanding and knowledge anchored in belief systems which underly our management education practices, social relations, and institutions.

The process of identifying beliefs has come from an iterative and grounded process of surveying published scholarship in the institutions that comprise the three leading journals. This process uncovers social relations between three different approaches to management education, built on rational pragmatism, radical poststructuralism, and divine metaphysics. The worlds which characterise these belief systems emerge by what are referred to here as schools, identified as: (1) the Rational School; (2) the Critical School; and (3) the Postliberal School.

First, there is the Rational School. Filled with tinkerers in the vein of Henry Ford or Steve Jobs, the Rational School embraces a rational empirical approach of pragmatism and evolutionary consequentialism to build student skills for a world of work. Rational scholars engage in a craft of improvement as management educators, always seeking to do better for their students and the corporations for whom they perform a production line role. As we shall see, this school has been the dominant one in management education in the pre-Millennium period, but it is now possible to argue scholarship in this style is fading.

Second, there is the Critical School. Composed of rebels in the mould of Luke Skywalker and Princess Leia from the *Star Wars* movies (Lucas, 1977), the Critical School embraces a radical poststructuralism to emancipate the student from the oppressive neoliberal corporation. Educators in this school seek to disrupt the hegemony of exploitative western ethnocentric institutions by exposing dominant power structures and pushing for equity. The dominant school in scholarship of the post-Global Financial Crisis period, there is a suggestion that this style of scholarship might be ascendent to the extent that it could crowd out other perspectives from the field.

Finally, there is the Postliberal School. Composed of fools in the mould of Don Quixote (De Cervantes, 1605), Ignatius J. Reilly from *A Confederacy of Dunces* (Toole, 1980), or George Costanza from *Seinfeld* (David & Seinfeld,

1989–1998), the Postliberal School presents an anti-scientism and an affinity with divine metaphysical traditions to emphasise formation of student being. Educators in this school are concerned with enabling the character of the student and searching for bonds of deeper common humanity in reviving institutions such as the family, community, and nation. A school which throughout the history of the management education field has been at its periphery, there is reason to suggest its status is currently near extinction.

The intention of exploring the three schools is to situate their complementary and oppositional relational attributes for presenting an understanding of that which might be defined as intellectually established and culturally legitimate within management education (Ringer, 1990). The process is also by way of provoking possible research questions and agendas which interested management education scholars may pursue in furthering the intellectual field.

AN INVITATION TO THE READER

The central premise of this book is that the best way to advance the future of management education research is to develop and nurture scholars who take a fascination and a delight in the field itself. Management education has typically been a 'second career'. It can be seen as the adjunct field of enquiry on which scholars occasionally depart from their discipline-specific scholarship to target work which might serve as part of a well-rounded academic career. Or sometimes it is viewed as a field of enquiry into which scholars stumble because of falling into a teaching focused career.

Training in the field seems rare. I recently attended a doctoral consortium at an international conference with a management education focus. Of approximately 30 doctoral students assembled, none was undertaking a PhD in management education. Many had attended via scholarship provided by the conference organisation, with several informing me that their institution would never have allowed them to participate if they had not been able to source such external funds. Similarly, I have recently joined a group of management educators seeking to pursue scholarly impact in their teaching and learning, and I reached out to someone I believed would be interested in joining the group. The person responded that they were in the process of trying to change from a Teaching Focused position to a Teaching and Research position at their institution, and that they therefore could not afford to be seen as a member of a management education group.

Yet, in business schools across the globe, virtually all of us teach. While there remains an attitude with some colleagues that time in the classroom represents time away from research, I still find many well-renowned disciplinary scholars who put significant time and effort into devising initiatives for their classroom. But many of them do not appear to consider the possibilities of publishing in management education. Why might this be the case?

My own reflections suggest that there is a gap between disciplinary knowledge, and knowledge in teaching and learning, and that many scholars feel the effort required to overcome this gap is too substantial. The disciplinary knowledge established through our doctoral studies requires such effort and ongoing maintenance and improvement that making the bridge to other fields of study such as management education can feel like a step too far. Teaching and research academics understand that the publishing process means engaging in a conversation with those who have come before them. Yet, as Huff (2016, p.241) contends, 'what is news in one conversation or subconversation is often of little interest to scholars in other areas of inquiry'. Tapping into the conversations that matter in management education is therefore an effort for those who want to publish. Those engaged in teaching-focused careers have a greater incentive to bridge this gap, yet they also often end up in a variety of administrative roles (Dean, 2018), where they can struggle to find time and space for migrating their scholarly knowledge beyond that of their PhD work into exploring the field of management education.

This book is therefore intended to advance the future of management education research by serving as a guide which will enable scholars to locate themselves within the intellectual field and publish in it. The message to readers is twofold. First, it is possible to bridge the gap between discipline-specific knowledge and management education knowledge. Indeed, the reader is likely to find underlying similarities between the beliefs and practices of management education and their own disciplinary field. Second, because management education represents a new field for many of us, there is much opportunity to make nuanced contributions by casting fresh eyes over its institutions, social relations, and practices.

To encourage the reader in this mission, each chapter closes with a series of reflective questions for prompting thoughts on how they might relate to the ideas and pedagogies they have encountered in their reading. The final chapter offers questions and areas of investigation on where scholarship might be advanced. It is hoped these prompts might enable the reader to locate themselves within the field and offer encouragement for them to undertake further exploration.

Before setting out this guide, it is worth briefly outlining my own management education journey. Having been appointed to a Teaching Focused position in 2018, my perspective is relatively new to the field. I feel grateful to have been invited to undertake Associate Editor roles at both JME and AMLE, to have worked with talented editors at both journals and engaged with insightful scholars in the Management and Organizational Behavior Teaching Society (MOBTS), and to have met passionate management educators at conferences around the globe. In the process of assuming these roles, I have also had to bridge the gap between disciplinary knowledge gained via a PhD thesis in organisation theory (Middleton, 2009), and extend to an understanding of management education (Huang et al., 2022). I am aware that the gap between two intellectual fields can seem daunting, but likewise, I think there are rewarding opportunities at hand for those prepared to dedicate themselves to taking this leap. Readers who engage with this book will find a richly diverse intellectual field and suggestions on topics and questions where they can make a valued contribution to advancing its knowledge. If this book prompts even one student to develop a fascination in the subject and to undertake a PhD in management education, then I will consider it to have been a worthwhile endeavour.

A BRIEF PREVIEW OF THE CONTENTS

This book proceeds as follows. Chapter 2 provides a brief orientation on the evolution of the field of management education. Harking back to views of management education as a 'lesser discipline' (Flexner, 1930), the chapter traces the 'business as science' approach to elevating the profession via Gordon and Howell (1959) and Pierson (1959). It then outlines the 1970s emergence of the precursor titles to ML and JME, and the creation and development of the MOBTS. The chapter notes ongoing tensions between research and teaching in business schools, the subsequent development of the practice of Scholarship of Teaching and Learning (Boyer, 1990), and the rise of the teaching-focused career (Bamber et al., 2017). Outlining the existential crisis for the management education profession prompted by the role that business graduates played in the 2008 Global Financial Crisis, this chapter traces the subsequent shift to a more Critical management education.

Chapter 3 provides a more extensive overview of the Rational School. Introducing the beliefs and practices of educators embedded in a rational pragmatic world of teaching and learning, the chapter traces a history of the dominant approach to management education scholarship and practice from the 1970s–1990s. This chapter examines how Rational educators have prepared students for the workplace by focusing on skill improvement to meet modern organisational needs, particularly in the area of technology. It also identifies a post-Millennium trend towards convergence with the Critical School in areas of ethics and identity.

Chapter 4 provides a more comprehensive introduction to the Critical School. Introducing beliefs and practices embedded in a world of radical post-structuralism, this chapter traces an approach which has expanded from a niche perspective confined to ML, to one which occupies the three main management education journals in the post-Millennium period. This chapter explores how critical educators have emancipated students from tradition by exposing power structures in western institutions, including the business school, through an emphasis on a rights-based ethics, disintegration of tradition, and advocacy of identity-based equity.

Chapter 5 delivers an introduction to the Postliberal School. Identifying a high point for this alternative approach during the mid-1990s, this chapter explores a perspective which now appears as an outlier in the intellectual field. Readers are introduced to a world of beliefs anchored in classical Roman and Greek traditions anchored in a divine metaphysical understanding of the world. This chapter sets out how Postliberal educators establish practices which provide parameters for students to explore their own character and enact frameworks for appreciating a deeper common humanity.

Leveraging the work set out in these chapters dedicated to the beliefs and practices of the individual schools, Chapter 6 then explores the social relations and institutions of the intellectual field. Maintaining the position that the best way to advance the future of management education is through developing scholars who take a fascination in the field, this chapter puts forward a series of prompts and questions for readers to consider their own relational position to scholarship in the area and identify how they might best contribute to thriving debate and scholarly conversation.

A FEW TECHNICALITIES

Before we begin, it is worth declaring some of the decisions which have had to be made in compiling this work. First, the research process which has been followed is an inductive and a grounded one, circulating incrementally between published scholarship in the field, and wider intellectual traditions (Glaser & Strauss, 1999). The prime sources of data for this search have been articles published in the field's three leading journals, AMLE, ML, and JME. As topics and themes have emerged through this process, they have prompted engagement with scholarship from outside the field. For example, work by Vaill (1996) and Harvey (1979) on learning as a way of being led to Carlin's (2021a) wider educational engagement with the same topic, which then subsequently prompted discovery of the work of Del Noce (Del Noce & Lancellotti, 2015) on limits and authority in education, and then re-engagement with the management education literature to discover work by Akin (1984) on authority in experiential learning.

Second, in compiling archival material on which to base this book the emphasis has been on where management education research has most often found a home. This has meant that my search has overwhelmingly been informed by that which has been published in ML, JME, and AMLE, the bastions of scholarly publishing in the field. This approach does not dismiss that other outlets have addressed issues of management education. For example, *Journal of Management Inquiry* with its investigations on teaching strategy as practice (Jarzabkowski & Whittington, 2008a) appears to have been a leader in investigating this topic. However, such themes appear to have found their way to be reflected in the leading management education journals (e.g. Feldman & Worline, 2016). While recognising that there is a wider literature at play, it therefore does not appear unreasonable to claim that the three leading journals provide a reasonable snapshot of what has comprised scholarly research in the field.

Third, it is not suggested that the Rational, Critical, and Postliberal schools provide an exhaustive list of approaches to management education. Indeed, I am aware of what might be described as a process-relational approach (e.g. Allan, 2012; Evans, 1998). However, with seemingly only a single entry in the management education journals (Chiles, 2003), it is possible to argue that this endeavour has not yet influenced the wider intellectual field. I therefore leave it to others to investigate such an approach. In reflecting on what is contained here, I am comfortable to say that when the worlds of the Rational, Critical, and Postliberal schools are expanded, they seem to account for much of the field's scholarly work. While these schools may therefore not be exhaustive, from my overview on what has been published there seems little in the field of management education which falls outside their combined broad approach.

Fourth, distinctions presented between the three schools are also somewhat artificial. On hearing an early version of this work at a presentation, one colleague asked whether it is possible to be both Rational and Critical? Of course, the answer is yes. In fact, one of the main arguments contained here is that there appears to be an increasing blurring of distinctions between the Rational and Critical schools. However, differentiation between the schools is important for illustrative purposes and for contemplating the future of scholarship in the management education field. While some colleagues in our profession will remain firmly rooted in one type of approach, others are likely to be more flexible. Readers should therefore keep in mind that distinctions between the schools are somewhat arbitrary. Chapter 6 will put forward the case that one important future contribution to shaping scholarship is likely to come from a more targeted treatment of social relations between schools in the management education field.

Fifth, there are also subgroups of these broader schools. For example, it would be possible to split the Critical School into more and less radical (Large-C Critical versus small-c critical) positions. While others are encouraged to devote greater attention to understanding each specific school and its underlying foundations, it is beyond the scope of a book attempting to take a lens to the wider management education field and its prospects. Such detail would also negate efforts in later chapters to explore juxtapositions and contraditions between the three schools as a basis for exploring a possible future for management education research. The positions outlined for each of the three schools demonstrate a sense of shared philosophy but must inherently recognise that none of the schools presents absolutely uniform perspectives. The intention in this work is therefore no more than to provide a flavour of each school.

Finally, it is important to note that the history presented on each of the schools is not intended to be 'complete'. The emphasis is on interpretive history, rather than history as fact. Any history presented here is necessarily potted, incomplete, and filled with my own interpretations. Over the past decade, the Critical School has done much to disavow any such overarching narratives (e.g. Prieto et al., 2021; Woods et al., 2022). However, the histories are intended to identify published scholarship which appears to have been important in setting an agenda for that which has come after it in the field. It would be likely that another author would devise histories comprising different key published outputs and topics. In that the field is likely to be advanced by such debates, this type of scholarship is warmly encouraged. For the moment, the reader should keep in mind that the composition of articles contained herein is my own construction of what has come before and what appears to have been important in management education.

On engaging with this book, the reader is encouraged to keep these technicalities in mind. Next, a brief introduction to the field of management education is provided.

QUESTIONS FOR THE READER

1. When you think of attempting to publish scholarship in management education, what is most likely to hold you back? Write down your top three reasons.
2. Determine how these three reasons will guide your reading of the rest of this book. Do they indicate a more targeted reading of any specific sections? Looking at the index, identify which sections might provide for greater consideration and make note of them.
3. Miss Scatcherd, Miss Honey, Jean Brodie, and Pangloss are some of the teachers who have been portrayed in classic literature. Who is your favourite teacher as depicted in popular literature, film, and other cultural works? What characteristics do you admire about this teacher? Are these same characteristics reflected in your own teaching?

2. A brief introduction to the field of management education

The widespread development of organisations in the late nineteenth century, followed by the rise in the 1950s of US corporations such as General Motors and Exxon Mobil expanding into global markets (Kay, 2019), created demand within the American institutional context for business schools. This context serves as the backdrop for much of what has subsequently happened in management education. While more recent critical interpretations suggest the rise of the business school was not solely a US-dominated affair (Wanderley et al., 2021), it remains the case that there is also a line of scholarship which laments the influence of US-style education on business schools and education more broadly (e.g. Tikkanen, 2023). This chapter traces the development of the management education field from the rise of business schools at University of Pennsylvania and Harvard, through to the Ford and Carnegie reports of 1959, the 1970s launch of *Management Learning* (ML) and *Journal of Management Education* (JME), the rise of the teaching-focused profession in the 1990s, and the post-Millennium turn towards a more critical scholarly approach.

LEGITIMATING THE FIELD

Overarching histories of management education often start by charting the rise of the business school. While early business education found some contemporaries in Europe (Redlich, 1957), it was in the United States where the idea of educating people formally for a career in business took hold. Prominent among these efforts was the establishment of business schools in eminent institutions such as Harvard, the University of Chicago, and the University of Pennsylvania. Courtesy of a US$100,000 donation to the University of Pennsylvania in 1881 to start a school of finance and economy, Joseph Wharton is held as the founder of this educational vision. An industrial pioneer, Wharton (1875) believed in national economies as a form of patriotism and in need of self-protection. Important to this system would therefore be the creation of a 'new class of university educated businessmen [*sic*]', whose vocational training would enable them to 'manage practical problems' (Khurana, 2007, p.106).

Leon C. Marshall, the fourth Dean of the Booth School of Business at the University of Chicago from 1909–1924, was one of the most active figures in establishing the template for how this new area of education should be recognised. Calling for 'experiments' to arrive at the ideal type of how the business curriculum should come together, Marshall (1921) put the case for an education based around specialist features of the organisation, including administration of personnel, market structures (e.g. sales, advertising, and relationships in manufacturing), finance, production, risk-bearing, and business unit structure. Business schools therefore started to organise courses along these lines of specialist business fields, with academic departments intended to parallel those of a business in areas such as marketing, finance, and accounting (McFarland, 1959). An example of the type of course which emerged from this functional specialisation was the introduction by Harvard in 1914–1915 of a subject in Factory Management.

The dominant pedagogical theme for these new centres of education was to prepare students for the workforce. Robert Calkins, Dean of the School of Business at Columbia University, reflected in a 1946 speech to the Association of Collegiate Schools of Business that 'the task in business education is to develop the competence of students for lifetime careers in the management of business and economic affairs'. According to Calkins, if management education did not 'give students a command of knowledge and the skill to use it in their own lives', then 'we have not educated them' (1946, p.46).

An important development for business school education in this post-World War II period was the way in which organisations had begun to evolve. Industrial firms such as General Electric and Standard Oil were now of a size where they began to dominate their industries. As firms grew, their reliance on a workforce comprising specialists structured according to small divisions began to wane. Large and multi-faceted departments started to emerge, led by generalist workers, whose capabilities created flexibility for moving across functional areas to meet new organisational challenges. This change created demand for universities to produce a more general type of manager (Colby et al., 2011).

However, this shift in workplace demand was a challenging one for business schools to meet. The shift to a generalist manager undermined the functional lines along which the earliest business schools had been established and brought business education to 'a significant crossroad' (McFarland, 1959). The trend was exacerbated by developments in Executive Education, where Harvard's Advanced Management Program (AMP) represented a leading attempt to bring tertiary education to new groups of students (Amdam & Benito, 2022).

However, perhaps the greatest challenge for business schools was an image which had taken hold in the university and wider society of management education as a lesser discipline. Prominent among these critics was educational reformer Abraham Flexner, who did not believe that business was a true profession. According to Flexner, business education compared unfavourably to disciplines such as law and medicine because it was not 'intellectual in character' (Flexner, 1930, p.164). Business scholars turning a spotlight on their own profession also noted disparities between the prominence of Frederick Winslow Taylor's scientific approach to management in the curriculum and the often-unscientific nature of educational practices.

These lines of thought came to a head in the late 1950s. The new *Journal of the Academy of Management* was published in 1959, and the topic of management education featured in the inaugural edition. Advocating the need for a 'discipline' of business administration, Goelz (1958) called for the profession to uncover and formulate broad principles and procedures of management which would provide the launchpad for 'young minds' to enter business administration. The culmination of this stream of thinking famously resulted in the release of the Ford and Carnegie reports on the future of management education.

The Ford Foundation Report, *Higher Education for Business*, was authored by Robert Gordon, Professor of Economics from the University of California, Berkeley, and James Howell, Associate Professor of Economics at the Graduate School of Business, Stanford. The investigation was premised on an argument that 'the vocational approach that has all too often characterized these schools [of business administration] in the past is now considered inadequate' (Gordon & Howell, 1959, p.v). Gordon and Howell's remit was substantial, even extending to questions on whether the business curriculum might better belong outside the university context. Eventually, the authors concluded in favour of a management sciences approach to education.

Noting that organisations had evolved towards more rational quantitative forms of decision making, the authors concluded that business education would need to become more scientific.

> It should recognize that businessmen [*sic*] in the decades ahead will need a higher order of analytical ability, a more sophisticated demand of analytical tools, a greater degree of organizational skill, a greater capacity to deal with the external environment of business, and more of an ability to cope with rapid change than has been true in the past. (Gordon & Howell, 1959, p.127)

For Gordon and Howell, the scientific turn in business demanded undergraduate degrees based on a structure including managerial accounting and statistics, advanced economics, organisation and administration, courses in the functional fields (marketing, etc.), some work on the legal, political, and social environment of business, and a capstone course in business policy.

Importantly, the report argued against the prevailing functional approach to business education of which Flexner had been so critical. Noting corporate demands for a more generalist graduate, Gordon and Howell concluded that business schools should 'require no "field of concentration" at all' (Gordon & Howell, 1959, p.135).

Pierson's (1959) *The Education of American Businessmen* [*sic*] represents the Carnegie Foundation's report on the state of business school education. Led by Swarthmore Professor of Economics, Frank C. Pierson, the report supported Gordon and Howell's argument for a more generalist business education based on scientific methods and techniques. Such an approach would require business scholars to develop a curriculum focused on developing student skills in 'clear analysis, imaginative reasoning, and balanced judgment' (Pierson, 1959, p.xiii). Pierson supported Gordon and Howell's move away from subject matter focused on high specialisation, because 'employers tend to look for qualities of integrity, vigor, resourcefulness, and general intelligence in new recruits' (Pierson, 1959, p. xiii). In pointing to a future for management education, Pierson concluded that the field should not respond to demands for 'knowledge of a highly detailed, technical nature', and instead encouraged generalist studies based on 'considerable analytical content' (Pierson, 1959, p.149).

The challenge for business schools was that a scientific approach to management education would also require a greater professionalisation of the workforce. Gordon and Howell's characterisation of the vocational approach to teaching as primarily descriptive had culminated in the view that the prevailing approach to tuition 'may help the student to land his [*sic*] first job, [but] is likely to handicap him [*sic*] in adjusting to new situations and in demonstrating his [*sic*] capacity to advance to more responsible positions' (Gordon & Howell, 1959, p.138).

Where retired professionals and others of a vocational bent had once comprised the population of educators in the business school, a new demand arose for faculty capable of bringing analytical acumen to bear on the organisation and its challenges. For Gordon and Howell this workforce adjustment meant that instructors in specialist areas of knowledge would require retraining in 'the use of more rigorous analytical tools', while some business schools would need to 'wait on the resignation, death, or retirement of key faculty members' (Gordon & Howell, 1959, p.141).

On a wider level, the push for a more scientific understanding of the management profession had a negative impact on the teaching of management education. Lewicki (1975, p.20) prophetically identified the 'significant 'gap' between increased demand for strong teaching competence – particularly at the MBA and undergraduate levels – and the increasing focus on research excellence in order to graduate from a doctoral programme and be promoted at most universities. Business schools therefore channelled bright and emerging minds into research-focused careers, and established performance targets which would discourage interest in teaching.

To the extent that faculty engaged in teaching, their task came to be educating students on the frameworks developed by the research of their peers in the business school. Hence, the propagation of apparently Rational frameworks for analysing business, such as the PESTEL Framework (Aguilar, 1967), Porter's Five Forces (1979), or the Resource-Based View of the Firm (Barney, 1991). Publish or perish became the mantra of business schools, where a narrative took hold of the scholar as a 'heroic workaholic publishing machine' (Harley, 2019, p.293). Under this schema, time in the classroom came to be viewed as wasted time, where the typical university 'hopes that professors will not neglect their teaching responsibilities but rewards them almost entirely for research and publications' (Kerr, 1975, p.773).

SCHOLARSHIP OF TEACHING AND LEARNING

The existential crisis this situation perpetuated for the management educator is captured by Fukami (2007) in a recount of her own career. Reflecting on her 'dirty little secret' that she was good at, and enjoyed, teaching, Fukami recalls a performance appraisal conversation with her department chair at a research-intensive institution. Reflecting on her submission of a conference paper to the 1979 Organizational Behavior Teaching Conference (OBTC), her department chair asked in a performance appraisal meeting whether she considered the presentation to be research or teaching. Fukami recollects:

> I didn't know how to answer him. In my heart, I knew that the presentation was about teaching. But in my head, I knew that was not the right answer, at least for that college. Wasn't I performing an important function for my college in being an effective teacher? Wasn't my effective teaching somehow correlated with my effectiveness as a researcher? Why did I have to choose one road over another? Why couldn't I be scholarly about teaching? (Fukami, 2007, p.360)

Into this scholarly educational void came two new journals. While the *Journal of Education for Business* had been inaugurated in 1928 with the ambition of keeping 'the reader informed on the activities in his [*sic*] field of endeavor; to let him know what the other school and the other executive or teacher is doing: why they are doing it, and how' (Haire, 1928, p.5), it was the establishment of ML in 1970 and the JME in 1975 which brought a renewed focus on management education.

Management Education and Development (since 1994, ML) emerged from a newsletter produced by the Association of Teachers of Management (ATM). Led by academics from UK business schools, the journal was important for bringing a non-US perspective to management education and emphasising a Critical approach to teaching. In the foreword to the first edition, Derek Pugh outlined the aim of the ATM and the journal as being 'to enable management teachers to contribute to the policies and practices of the profession, and by so doing to raise its quality and effectiveness wherever it is carried out' (Pugh, 1970, p.1). A glimpse of the Critical flavour of ML is captured in the first issue by Scott's characterisation of the firm as 'a political entity', and the need for developing 'an awareness of this aspect of business life among those ... operating from a position of weakness in respect of authority' (Scott, 1970, p.60).

Across the Atlantic came the 1975 launch of the journal, *The Teaching of Organization Behavior* (since 1991, JME). Emerging from a collection of 14 US business schools comprising the Organizational Behavior Teaching Society, the aim of the journal was to share teaching approaches and innovations developed by faculty at member institutions. In its lead editorial, Founding Editor David Bradford set out the goal 'to keep this journal as uncomplicated as possible and devote it to teaching techniques and theory rather than making it another research publication. Somebody suggested, jokingly, that any article with extensive empirical data or a reference list longer than six items should be rejected' (Bradford, 1975a, p.2). Over a near 50-year history, JME has primarily published Rational School scholarship. However, it is possible to discern a Postliberal School flavour in early editions, while the post-Millennium period has seen the journal take on a more Critical bent.

New external forces also began to reshape the practice of management education. Whereas the 1959 Carnegie and Ford reports had been a response to the growing market demand for generalist managers, new educational imperatives came to the fore as the corporation was supercharged by macroeconomic reforms of deregulation implemented by western governments in the 1980s. Driven by inflationary and employment problems in the United States and the United Kingdom, Ronald Reagan and Margaret Thatcher undertook a series of market-based policy reforms aimed at deregulating competition and encouraging the flow of private capital. Inspired by economists at the Chicago School of Economics, this neoliberal approach to state-based policy held that perfect markets offered the path to a free society and would provide answers to social ills. Liberating corporations from government regulation would unleash the variety and diversity of individual genius for enabling great civilisation advances (Friedman, 2002).

This neoliberal approach held that the role of government was not to determine winners and losers. Markets could achieve social cohesion based on a drip-down economics of growth where everybody could win from growing the size of the pie to share. Neoliberal economists also turned attention towards education. One implication of their thinking was that the state should be removed from resourcing decisions which favoured state-based education over the market. Instead, full independence and diversity would be best enabled by a market-based competition which would allow private colleges and universities to flourish, therefore providing impetus for a higher standard of scholarship (Friedman, 2002).

Not only did this market-based mantra fuel substantial growth in the corporation, it also had the effect of corporatizing the modern university and, by association, the business school. The efficiency agenda of the market became prominent in higher education institutions. Rewards and sanctions based on publishing research became prominent, with implications for surviving and thriving in the business school through maximising output (Jones et al., 2020). This system imperilled the good teacher who performed their craft with expertise, but without scholarly productivity.

Recognising that this emerging paradigm posed a threat to those of a more educational bent, Carnegie Foundation President Ernest Boyer published a model of scholarship which sought to move beyond a research versus teaching dichotomy. Noting that a love for teaching had drawn many academics to universities, Boyer (1990) argued that the pervasive research and publication culture in business schools restricted creativity in the profession and led to poorer educational outcomes. Boyer therefore introduced the idea of a scholarship of teaching. This approach treated faculty not just as teachers, but also as learners committed to creating a common ground of intellectual commitment. Teaching would no longer mean just transmitting knowledge to students, but 'transforming and extending it as well' (Boyer, 1990, p.24).

Fukami (2007) speaks of the scholarship of teaching as 'the third road', a career which balances somewhere between a research career and a teaching career. Following a third road career means understanding scholarship as the discovery and creation of new knowledge, the application of this knowledge to solve real problems, the integration of scholarship to merge knowledge across disciplinary boundaries, and the dissemination of knowledge through teaching. One corollary of this new line of thinking was the rise in management education of the teaching-focused profession.

Into this new world of scholarship in 2002 emerged the *Academy of Management Learning and Education* (AMLE). Recommended by a taskforce at the 1996 Academy of Management for the Academy to 'publish high-quality materials on management learning, education, and teaching for its members …', the mission of AMLE was to present 'theory, models, research, critique, dialogues, and restrospectives that address the learning process and enhance the practice of education in the management disciplines' (Lewicki, 2002, p.8). The entry of the Academy into the field of management education was an important moment. As the most prestigious body of business school academics, it had long been associated with the publish or perish mantra. The launch of AMLE meant the Academy now recognised scholarship in teaching and learning as a genuine area of study.

CORPORATE COLLAPSE AND MANAGEMENT EDUCATION

However, external forces were again to disrupt the field of management education. The fall of Enron and Arthur Andersen in the early 2000s, followed by the Global Financial Crisis of 2007 and 2008 brought much introspection on what management education should look like (Whittington et al., 2003). While governments bailed out the investment bankers who had precipitated these crises, many regular people lost their livelihoods and homes. The situation was not lost on management educators that many of those who had acted improperly in the financial sector were esteemed business school graduates. Increasingly, management educators asked if the education system in which they worked was to blame (Ghoshal, 2005). To the extent that the US postgraduate system had played a role in educating the global banking elite, many in the wider management field answered this question in the affirmative (Kerr & Robinson, 2012). These critics felt that for too long business education had promoted an understanding that the purpose of business was to make profits for its owners and had neglected any social purpose for the enterprise (Friedland & Jain, 2020).

The result has prompted a turn against business school education from within. Two main implications of this existential crisis have emerged. The first is a more concerted turn towards the Critical School, and efforts to expose values and orientations in management education perceived as 'tacitly serving the maintenance of economic systems based upon market competition and the interests of the people in charge of organizations – while appearing to be neutral and value-free' (Learmonth, 2007, p.109). This Critical turn seems apparent in each of the main journals. Where the Critical School had previously only featured in ML, similar perspectives now take hold in JME where Marxist terms such as hegemony are adopted (Neal & Finlay, 2008), and at AMLE where greater interest in upending historical narratives around the development of management education field is established (Cummings & Bridgman, 2011). AMLE also turns a focus on business schools themselves as neoliberal enterprises (McLaren et al., 2021).

The second feature of the introspection the Global Financial Crisis prompted for management education is a pedagogical one. A renewed pedagogy has emerged which offers a turn away from instruction based on models and frameworks associated with positivist empirics and emphasises more interpretive management practices. The thinking appears to be that if the Global Financial Crisis and other associated corporate ethical violations represent a failure of managers to question taken-for-granted values instilled by the management education system, then teaching the mundane everyday practice of managerial activity might enable students to recognise and challenge bad practice (Jarzabkowski & Whittington, 2008b). Hence, the pedagogical push for strategy as practice as a technique designed to provoke student recognition and reflection on what it means to be a competent management practitioner (Jarzabkowski & Whittington, 2008b). Further acknowledgement of this practice turn in the management education field comes in 2016 with the launch of a new journal, *Management Teaching Review* (MTR). Dedicated to 'challenging management educators to continuously explore and improve our craft ...' (Forray & Dean, 2016, p.4), MTR has established an outlet for practice-based management education scholarship.

In 2011, the Carnegie Foundation again weighed in on the future of management education. *Rethinking Undergraduate Business Education: Liberal learning for the profession* (Colby et al., 2011) returned to Abraham Flexner, and his view that a broad education in the liberal arts should comprise the background of any student. According to Flexner, this education would provide the basis for active citizenship in a democratic society. In considering the challenges of understanding the role of business education within the social world and fostering the ability of students to improve public prosperity and well-being on the back of their studies, Colby and colleagues declare that 'business education must be integrated with liberal learning' (2011, p.4). The authors believe that liberal learning will enable students to draw on varied points of knowledge and address issues from multiple points of view, thereby encouraging responsible engagement with the world. This liberal arts turn has driven interest in a range of different experiential approaches to the classroom, where creative experimentation using theatre, visual arts, music, dance, and choreography now occupy established approaches in management education (Barry & Meisiek, 2015).

CONCLUSION

So, where next for management education research? Reflecting on this very brief history of the evolution of the management education field, we can see development from a vocational field towards one which now encourages a scholarly approach to the research and practice of teaching. Signposts such as calls from the Ford and Carnegie foundations for a more scientific approach to management education, the rise of ML and JME in the 1970s, the rise of the scholarship of teaching in the 1990s, and the more Critical turn prompted by neoliberal financial failures in the post-Millennium period, have all prompted change for management education research.

What this history hints at is a field characterised by different approaches to management education. Research in the scientific era adopted more rational empirical scholarship than in the post-Millennium period, where the rising liberal arts and practice-based perspective has integrated more interpretive Critical scholarship. This evolution does not suggest a fragmented field. But it does suggest that there are important differing philosophical foundations underlying our approaches to management education, and that these will be important to what is studied in the field and how this scholarship is undertaken.

To engage in this discussion, the next three chapters present overviews of the three identified schools. Consistent with Bourdieu's (1969) notion of an intellectual field, the chapters are split into sections which focus on the worlds of beliefs and practices which comprise the three schools. The first section of each chapter draws attention to underlying beliefs of the relevant school, focusing on their inherent philosophies.

When it comes to practices, subject matter is clustered according to how each school relates to the corporation. The argument here is that how management educators relate to the for-profit corporation (as opposed to other entities such as not-for-profits, or government entities) is essential to how individual educators place themselves within the intellectual field and serves as a key influence on their classroom approach.

Support for the position that management education is defined by its position relative to the corporation is brought to the fore by early editions of each of the three leading journals, where definitions of organisation might now be applied to the corporate form which has subsequently risen to prominence. In the opening piece for ML, Pugh argues 'we still have a long way to go in understanding the management process and therefore in determining how best education may contribute to it' (Pugh, 1970, p.1). In the second editorial for JME, Bradford proposes a ten-year horizon for the teaching of Organizational Behaviour: 'what sort of managers will they [organisations] need and how should our graduate and undergraduate programs be adapted to fit these needs' (1975b, p.2)? Finally, Lewicki uses the first edition of AMLE to outline the central objective of the new journal as being 'to better support the improvement of management practice by improving management education' (2002, p.8).

Conceptually, organisations are 'stable associations of persons engaged in concerted activities directed to the attainment of specific objectives' (Bittner, 1965, p.239). Pulling apart this definition, we can identify three essential aspects of the organisation.

First, organisations produce things. Their concerted activities are directed towards involving people in the process of production, whether this involves relatively unskilled involvement in assembly line activities, or highly technical activities in production of services and knowledge-intensive goods (Berger et al., 1973). Second, organisations attain specific objectives. They determine their actions towards these objectives by their values, or global beliefs that 'transcendentally guide actions and judgments across specific objects and situations' (Rokeach, 1968, p.160). Finally, the individual is implicated in the definition of an organisation. Humans bring attitudes, impulses, wishes, and expectations to their work (Levinson, 1965). Organisations also become invested with psychological meaning for their members (Selznick, 1957).

Specifically, the three components of the definition of organisation suggest themes in management education around how the organisation produces, how it attains its objectives, and how it relates to the individual. In short, the definition implies a business education built around skills (how the organisation engages in production), ethics (how the organisation attains its objectives), and identity (how the organisation relates to the individual). The argument put forward in this book is that the way in which an individual educator sets their relationship to the for-profit corporation will define their role in the school in which they are embedded, the pedagogies they employ in their classroom, and the manner in which they explore issues related to skills, ethics, and identity.

The following three chapters therefore explore beliefs and practices of each of the three schools of management education. To begin this task, Chapter 3 provides an overview of the Rational School.

QUESTIONS FOR THE READER

1. Up until the late 1950s, management education was not considered a legitimate intellectual field by classical sciences, medicine, and law. To what extent do you think this situation maintains today?
2. The response by Gordon and Howell (1959) and Pierson (1959) to these claims of field-level illegitimacy was to push for a more empirical approach to education and teaching. In your view, has this approach met its intention?
3. Beyond an empirical approach, what do you think might be another way to achieve field-level legitimacy?
4. When you think about the Scholarship of Teaching and Learning, can you see elements of Fukami's (2007) 'third road' in your own career?
5. The journals ML, JME, and AMLE, each have their own different traditions and perspectives. Thinking of these journals, is there one you read more regularly than the others? Why?
6. This chapter links shifts in management education with several societal events such as market-based policy reforms of the 1980s, the fall of Arthur Andersen and Enron at the turn of the Millennium, and the Global Financial Crisis. Can you think of a societal event which has shaped your

own teaching? Why did this event resonate with you to the extent that you changed something in your classroom?

3. A brief (and incomplete) history of the Rational School

The tinkerer teacher surveyed her classroom. Something had not felt quite right. Her analytics dashboard told her student engagement with the textbook was low. Only 31 per cent of students had read the preparatory chapter for the day, and only 47 per cent had watched her introductory video. Would she lose their attention by introducing concepts at a more advanced stage than for which they were prepared? And if they weren't tuning in, then how would they be prepared for the workplace? Today's topic was on strategic planning, and she knew that skills on analysing the organisation's internal and external environments were highly valued by prospective employers. If the tinkerer teacher had to guess, the students were all busy working, spending time with family, undertaking sporting commitments, and scrolling away at their social media. Their social media? That was it! Perhaps there was a way of introducing key concepts by using a social media platform? Maybe there were ways of reaching students on their own terms, at a time and via media which suited them? She pulled out her phone and started to search. Which platform should she use?

If the number of published articles provides a basis for determining the dominant school in management education, then the Rational School has been at the forefront of the field. Scholars in this school perceive education as playing a key role in providing for engines of capital. Pierson captured this style of thinking in the Carnegie Report, when he depicted the business system as 'the principal source of material progress in this country …' and outlined a national imperative for management education in 'maintaining the growth rate of the American economy' (Pierson, 1959, p.89). This imperative is reflected in Pierson's ambition to educate the American businessman (*sic*), with a focus on management development (Anderson et al., 2020).

From the 1970s to the 1990s, large segments of published works represented an approach to management education focused on developing student skills for the workplace. This type of scholarly contribution was perhaps most apparent in *Journal of Management Education* (JME), but has also featured in *Academy of Management Learning and Education* (AMLE), and to a lesser extent in *Management Learning* (ML).

In a metaphorical sense, the image of the educator in the Rational School can be seen as one of a tinkerer. The tinkerer is always about improvement. Making do with the resources at hand and recombining these for new purposes, the tinkerer looks for new ways to adapt resources and create opportunities (Chang & Rieple, 2018). Here, we can see Steve Jobs attending calligraphy class to change perceptions and find value in the previously unappreciated (Paton et al., 2014), or his refusal to accept limitations in stretching people to overcome challenges (Pina e Cunha et al., 2017). The tinkerer also captures the failure of Henry Ford's first two automotive ventures in providing 'the opportunity to begin again more intelligently' (Bolinger & Brown, 2014, p.452).

The world of the Rational School leads its scholars to the view that organisations have purposes, people have needs, and bringing the two together is both possible and desirable. Porter (1983) suggests the range of questions which drive Rational scholarship, including: (1) What competencies should be taught? (2) Where should these competencies be taught? (3) Who should teach the competencies and (4) How do we teach managerial competencies? In this school, educators graft away at honing different pedagogical techniques, always with their mind fixed on building the skills of their students for entering the workforce. According to this view, the task of management education is to prepare students for the 'real' world of work (Bilimoria, 1998). Tinkerers actively seek to piece together insights on what is happening in industry. Scrounging information from online and traditional media, industry relationships, publishers, colleagues, friends, and family, they assemble a picture of what is new and emerging in industry and attempt to reflect this understanding through their management education practice.

This ambition is captured by Boeble and Buchanan in their module on first-year Organizational Behaviour, and particularly their attempts to disabuse students of 'an unrealistic perception of the manager's job ... [resting] on the portrayal of managers by the popular media and their aspirations to be powerful decision-makers and leaders of men' (1975, p.29). The authors point to Mintzberg's (1975) studies on the nature of managerial work as the inspiration for their classroom practice around managers, a body of work which emphasises managerial skills in interpersonal relations based around peer relationships, negotiation, motivating subordinates, resolving conflicts, and establishing information networks. Central to these interpersonal roles is the capability of the manager to reconcile the individual needs of employees with the goals of the organisation.

The incrementalist nature of the tinkerer's profession means that pedagogy is a process of gradual improvement. Theirs is a world which doesn't require radical change, but one which needs refining. Metrics of student evaluations and other quantitative and qualitative data on the effectiveness of student learning can serve as the basis for honing their craft, but the Rational scholar is most driven towards improving their practice by observing the outcomes of their actions.

RATIONAL SCHOOL FOUNDATIONS

The Rational School is based on a philosophy of rational pragmatism, an ethics of evolutionary consequentialism, an embrace of the liberal, and an understanding of authority as the freedom to. These foundations are set out in Figure 3.1.

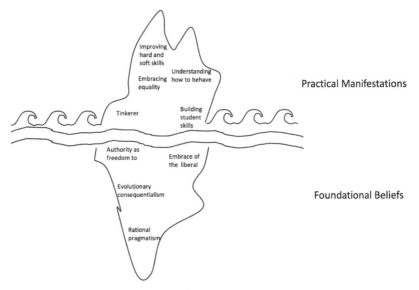

Figure 3.1   The world of the Rational School

The pragmatic approach is a philosophy which devolves from United States, where a suspicion of elite thought drove nineteenth- and early twentieth-century philosophers such as Charles Peirce, William James, and John Dewey to link knowledge and practice. It is important to note that when Joseph Wharton founded the first US business school, pragmatism was the prevailing philosophical position of the time. Despite attempts by Pierson (1959) and Gordon and Howell (1959) to impose a greater scientific empiricism upon management education, the pragmatic approach remains fundamental to the field today.

Often viewing philosophical ideals derived in Europe and ancient societies as pompous and pretentious, pragmatics argue that 'nothing new can ever be learnt by analyzing definitions' (Peirce, 2016, p.289). Instead, pragmatists view the world through a lens of 'effectiveness in action' (Joullie & Spillane, 2020, p.257). Two concepts essential to the pragmatic approach are therefore meaning and action, where meaning cannot be separated from action.

For pragmatists, truth represents an evolving quest which is based in action. Peirce puts forward the notion that ideas and beliefs are defined by their consequences. For example, what we believe to be wine is only wine because we know the qualities the wine possesses.

> Thus our action has exclusive reference to what effects the senses, our habit has the same bearing as our action, our belief the same as our habit, our conception the same as our belief; and we can consequently mean nothing by wine but what has certain effects, direct or indirect, upon our senses ... our idea of anything is our idea of its sensible effects. (Peirce, 2016, p. 294)

In a similar vein, James and Dewey continued to explore the relationship between action and knowing. For Dewey, the practical link between thinking and knowing means that the central goal of scientific discovery comes to be about growth, the 'constant reorganisation of human experience, the solution of practical problems and the resolution of conflicts' (Joullie & Spillane, 2020, p.266). One important consequence of the Rational School's pragmatism is an uneasy empiricism. The rejection of pure ideas by the pragmatists makes for an empirical scientific knowledge which is not adequate in and of itself. While the nature of evidence in the Rational School is often based around techniques which are verifiable and replicable such as evidence-based management (Wright et al., 2018), it remains the case that particularly early work in management education presents pedagogical techniques that often have a practice basis but are less quantifiable (e.g. Cohen, 1975).

This empirical-pragmatic tension is witnessed in Dodge (1980), whose description of an evening on his favourite chair with a book and a blanket illustrates the dilemmas a Rational scholar faces between teaching around scientific enquiry, versus dressing up tentative conclusions into deterministic statements for students. The result is that while Rational scholarship has embraced Pierson (1959) and Gordon and Howell (1959) and claims to have an empirical approach to knowledge, its basis is often more pragmatic than the scientific standard encouraged by the Ford and Carnegie reports.

The practical evolutionary process of knowledge for pragmatists is also important to explaining the nature of ethics within the Rational School, a topic which Dewey regularly explored. Similar to their disdain for philosophical beliefs based on theoretical deduction, pragmatists also hold that value judgements must be based on human nature rather than a priori principles or divine interpretations. Dewey contends that a practice-based moral framework will not do away with ethical problems and perplexities, 'but it would enable us to state problems in such forms that action could be courageously and intelligently directed to their solution' (Dewey, 1930, p.13). The result of this style of thinking is a Rational School ethics which is based on evolutionary consequentialism, where morals and values emerge through patterns of behaviour and revised value judgements (Joullie & Spillane, 2020).

At the heart of pragmatism is a distinction between knowledge based on empirics and knowledge based on practice. The result is that pragmatists consider themselves to be people who believe in free will and are generally religious and optimistic, but they characterise scientific empiricists as people who reject free will and are generally irreligious and pessimistic people (Joullie & Spillane, 2020). At the heart of this distinction is an embrace by pragmatists of the liberal. Where empiricists give primacy to supreme authority of theories and moral laws, they 'produce vague, dull, halting and evasive observation of actual social ties' (Dewey, 1922, p.328). Pragmatists instead suggest that knowledge and morals must be based on 'a free will of arbitrary choice ... a non-empirical authority of right and a non-empirical conscience which acknowledges it' (Dewey, 1922, p.326).

Finally, an important distinction between the Rational and Postliberal schools and the Critical School rests in the idea of authority. To the Rationalist, authority is not something to be escaped. Rather, a manager's skills and abilities may make them authoritative – capable by their expertise of a cooperative style of management in which contributions of relevant colleagues are elicited and voluntarily made (Spillane & Joullie, 2021).

The foundations of the Rational School mean that the educator comes to think of their job as part of an assembly line, with their role being the production of students for the market enterprise. Rational scholars therefore develop educational initiatives to reflect what an organisation does, rather than to prompt thinking on what it might do. While Bradford poses the question in an early edition of JME on whether management educators should try to influence the future through their research and teaching (1975b), Rational School education has often been downstream of culture. The task of tinkerer teachers is therefore to evolve pedagogical techniques in response to societal and cultural change (Brannen, 1986). As we shall see, this approach means management education topics such as environmental sustainability or equity have often been developed in response to macro-environment trends and topics, rather than in advance of them. As we shall see, it is this largely impassive stance which draws criticism from the Critical School (e.g. Parker, 2018a).

To summarise, the Rational School is aimed at the improvement of management education and the management educator, as evidenced by its image of the tinkerer. The key task of the educator is a continual process of improving, which is achieved through building student skills. The basis of pedagogy is a practice-based one, and the basis of ethics is an evolutionary consequentialism of considering the results of actions. The result is an approach to management education which aims to improve student skills and provide understanding of how students should behave in the workplace, and an embrace of equality.

IMPROVING STUDENT SKILLS: HARD AND SOFT SKILLS FOR THE WORKPLACE

The Rational perspective means that the imperative for management educators is to provide students with the opportunity to think about and practise skills in specific encounters (Fink, 1979). The educational challenge in this approach is that many students, particularly at the undergraduate level, are yet to experience the world of work for which education is preparing them. Providing opportunity to experience management through 'hands-on' education therefore becomes a priority for educators in the Rational School (Miller, 1991). This imperative means that the history of the Rational School presents an evolution through pedagogies and approaches designed to replicate the challenges students will face in the workforce. Here we see techniques designed to bring organisational contexts to the student including the business case (Swierca & Ross, 2003), field research and consultation (Guest, 1976), role play (Randolph et al., 1976), and computer simulations (Solomon, 1979).

Student acquisition of technology-directed hard skills versus communication-directed soft skills has captured much attention in the Rational School's approach to management education. This debate is captured in much of the late 1950s context around the development of the field, where the Ford and Carnegie reports weighed up the merits of specialisation in areas such as technology, versus generalisation in soft skills such as communication, emotional maturity, decision making, and judgement (Gordon & Howell, 1959). This theme is also observed in seminal early pieces in organisation studies (e.g. Burns & Stalker, 1961). My discussion with founding figures in the Management and Organizational Behavior Teaching Society (MOBTS) even suggests that the society was formed in response to a perceived disdain for the teaching of soft skills from certain sections of the business school.

Turning first to technology, it is reasonable to suggest that tinkerer teachers have long been captured by its inherent possibilities. Given that the corporation seized on the technological revolution of the 1960s and 1970s, scholars in the Rational School tradition have been early adopters in teaching students to competently use computing technology. With computers perceived by the Rational School as a liberating agent (Miesing, 1998), tinkerers have long been encouraged to work closely with information systems scholars in curriculum planning to provide 'more computer-assisted instruction' (Ready, 1975, p.17).

One popular pedagogy has been to leverage computer simulations as a broadly applicable approach for mimicking the complex and changing world of organisations (Wheelwright, 1972, p.154). An early example of this approach in management education is detailed by George Washington University Professor, George Solomon (1979), whose experience in using the Digital PDP-11 interactive computer to simulate situations and dilemmas was designed for improving student skills in interpersonal competence. Solomon's program posed 22 questions/dilemmas to students in which they were required to answer from a sample vocabulary. The computer then rated the individual's response in determining whether a competent or incompetent response had been provided. The program was designed to improve student learning by enabling them to repeat the dilemma and correct mistakes made in their previous responses.

However, while Solomon presents a ground-breaking pedagogy its application also required a level of computing expertise likely to have been beyond many of his faculty peers at the time. As a result, the realm of computers tended to be isolated in specialist areas of the university. By 1985, the push in management education was to move computers away from computer science departments and engage with broader integration into the business school (Hope & Higgins, 1985). Noting the dramatic growth in the use of microcomputers in Fortune 500 firms, Dyer (1987) argued it was important for business students to develop expertise in information management, information analysis, and decision analysis. In an influential book on the future of management education, Porter and McKibben (1988) recommended that business schools embed a computer-enabled information orientation across the curriculum.

A study on microcomputer usage in major corporations by Rogers et al. (1988) suggests the types of skills students would require in this changing environment and offers thoughts on where such competencies should be brought into educational pathways. The authors suggest technological literacy would stem from skills taught at the high school level such as keyboarding, computer operation, operating systems, and programming. The advice from Rogers and colleagues is that remedial work should only be undertaken at college level if the student is not proficient in these areas. According to this perspective, the focus of business school education should instead be on using relevant exercises and case work to hone student skills in applications including word processing, spreadsheets, databases, statistical applications, data collection, mapping, and bibliometric searching (Rogers et al., 1988).

However, by the 1990s, rapid improvements in computing power had developed at a pace which enabled organisations to improve the decision-making performance of their managers. Such developments suggested that students would require new types of technological skills. These advances meant students should be educated in software designed for analysing business case problems (DuBrin, 1992). This development saw management education journals present reviews on decision-aiding software, to help guide the tinkerer on the most appropriate tool to integrate into their classroom (Power et al., 1993).

The internet revolution in the mid-1990s meant that distinctions between computer skills and other types of skills in the business curriculum were soon to become less pronounced. The World Wide Web not only provided new ways for organisations to conduct business online, it also offered novel ways for universities to reach their students and teach them. Technological progression enabled instructors to link classes at different universities or campuses and create virtual classrooms, provide new ways to facilitate student participation, and provide students with the opportunity to practise key technological workplace skills (Treadwell et al., 1998). Students could now undertake learning at a distance, they brought laptops to class, and they communicated with each other through electronic means. CD-ROM and other multimedia enabled computer-assisted methods for exploring business cases (Bilimoria, 1999). Importantly, internet-enabled education broke down the distinction between technological skills and other types of skills because it required students to develop technical skills at the same time as they were applying them.

With the rise of the smartphone and social media, the post-Millennium period has continued to provide educators and students with new ways of engaging with management education. Given that corporations have applied such technology in developing their own markets and students have enthusiastically adopted these platforms in their own personal lives, such applications present opportunities for tinkerers to not only provide students with workplace skills but also to drive learner engagement. Students are now presented with courses designed to build their skills in applying technologies such as LinkedIn (Gerard, 2012), Wikis (Daspit & D'Souza, 2012), X (formerly Twitter) and Facebook (Lim et al., 2014), and Pinterest (Schmidt, 2016). Management education now also provides opportunities for students to use technical tools applied in organisations to facilitate data- and metrics-driven approaches to decision making (Schwarz & Murphy, 2008).

This leap to technology-enabled instruction has been given further impetus by the COVID-19 pandemic. Perhaps concerned at becoming pedestrians on the information superhighway (Bilimoria, 1997, p.234), some faculty leading into the pandemic had previously held out against integrating technology into their pedagogy. However, lockdowns and social distancing demanded that faculty throw away any enduring remnants of techno-scepticism. If an academic wanted to maintain their career, online teaching became the only approach for achieving it. During this period, blended, hybrid, and fully online delivery replaced the face-to-face on-campus instruction which had always been the means of delivery for higher education (Rivers & Holland, 2022). Teachers were able to experiment with different types of technology for reaching students in new ways as they dealt with a cohort often unable to leave their homes and dealing with a range of previously unimagined social and educational pressures. Here, faculty leveraged applications such as TikTok for providing students with bite-sized educational content (Middleton, 2022).

New technologies promise further possibilities for the future of management education. An emerging area of interest for the Rational School is in skills-based building for the Fourth Industrial Revolution (4IR). This period of artificial intelligence (AI) and machine learning is seen as likely to cause disruption in ways that will fundamentally alter the way in which work is done (Fukami et al., 2022). Such technologies promise the personalisation of learning at a mass scale, leveraging a student's learning profile to enable a precision education with personalised learning journeys for meeting individual career objectives (Lefevre & Caporarello, 2022). Leveraging these new technologies means that feedback can be provided to students in ways which are most effective to them. Some students might require one-on-one sessions, others via email. The technological tools of the twenty-first century can assist the Rational educator to tap into what motivates a learner and engage with them in ways which are unique to the individual (Rivers & Holland, 2022).

In anticipating what the future of technology might represent for management education, the main question for Rational scholars would seem to be the extent to which technology should be integrated into teaching. Here, it is worth reflecting on earlier work by Cohen and Lippert (1999) which identifies a continuum on the application of technology in management education, from a technology-free classroom, through to complete reliance on it. Their conclusion that 'technology should facilitate the learning process, not dictate it' (Cohen & Lippert, 1999, p.744) seems to reach a position on limits of integration into management education. However, the suggestion that AI will provide personalised responsive learning at a large scale (Rivers & Holland, 2022) perhaps opens greater temptation to new and more subtle types of technological intervention in learning. At the least, developments in AI would suggest that students require new skills in technological savvy and predictive capacity (Fukami et al., 2022).

For the Rational School, use of technology appears to raise only minor ethical concerns. In what is a rare piece which addresses this topic, Allen (2020) acknowledges that teaching students about ethical issues associated with the cutting-edge technologies of the 4IR will be important in shaping their tech literacy. Citing the need for students to think critically about topics such as who has access to data and where it is stored, and the biases embedded within software and algorithms, he notes the importance of students in developing the mindset to explore such considerations prior to adopting a technological solution (Allen, 2020). It seems possible that the rise of AI software and the possibilities this may enable for students to cheat in their assessments might provoke tinkerers to reflect on their faith in technological advances. However, to date, Rationalists have taken the position that questions over technology are of degree, rather than of implementation.

A second emphasis for tinkers in improving student workplace skills has been in soft skills. The argument on the need for management educators to improve student soft skills is well established and is evidenced in the push in the 1950s towards a more generalist education for managers. Support for a soft skills approach is found in arguments by management gurus such as Henry Mintzberg (1975), who argues that management education is successful in training specialists such as researchers and accountants but is ineffective in teaching skills required by managers, such as resolving conflicts, motivating subordinates, and making decisions.

The soft skills perspective is prominent in both ML and JME, the latter of which has historically represented teachers in Organization Behaviour, where a bent for promoting better understanding on human motivation and behaviour features. Topics in this area have remained relatively consistent, including a focus on skills including capabilities in communication (Foote, 2013), leadership styles and their implications for how managers work (Durbrow, 1978), motivation of oneself and others (Siegall, 1988), management of team and organisational culture (Starr-Glass, 2004), and power (Akin, 1979). However, the approaches by which these topics have been taught have evolved.

Early approaches to teaching skills in communication include experiential exercises designed to facilitate understanding of non-verbal communication (Powers, 1975), and the adoption of videotape technology for recording and playing back student presentations to improve the quality of their verbal communication (Comte, 1980). By the 1980s, the implementation of group work in many management educations classes saw educators expand their interests in communication beyond that of perceiving it as a workplace skill and instead recognise the pedagogical capacity of communicative devices for improving student learning. Along these lines, techniques to feature in the classroom include course agreements to create a positive environment in which student communication would occur (Jenster & Duncan, 1987), and the establishment of writing communities to learn the process of organising and working within a group (LeVan, 1987). Soon, educators would develop roles such as student ombudsperson, where a student could practise a key workplace role at the same time as improving communication between the instructor and class (Herring & Mendleson, 1999). However, more recent innovations in student communication skill-building once again turn to technology (Foote, 2013; Ozcelik & Paprika, 2010).

When it comes to leadership styles, early approaches tend to focus on developing an inventory of behaviour (e.g. Veiga, 1978), or adapting experiential exercises such as Classroom As Organization (CAO) for teaching leadership skills (Cohen, 1976). By putting students into the position of an organisational member who must deal with genuine organisational problems, the CAO approach requires the selection of a group leader, who is then responsible for their group's performance and often also for evaluating the performance of individual members. Cohen asserts that in the CAO model, 'students probably learn as much from our classroom managerial behavior as they do from the content of our teaching' (1976, p.13). More recent approaches develop leadership behaviour through techniques such as the martial art of aikido (Clawson & Doner, 1996), setting up classroom activities where students speak to their peers as though they are a coach delivering a dramatic locker room talk (Linowes, 1992), and the use of more reflective techniques such as mindfulness (Donaldson-Feilder et al., 2022).

While motivation has been a key feature of Organizational Behaviour courses and has therefore been prominent in educational techniques (e.g. Siegall, 1988), Rational School scholars have also picked up on organisational efforts to engage in a growth mindset and have sought to replicate similar efforts in the classroom by engaging with leading techniques in areas such as neuroscience. These attempts include using advances in neuroscience to emotionally engage students in learning through material objects such as clay and LEGO® (Taylor & Statler, 2014), as well as to reduce defensive reaction to threats through improving skills in emotional intelligence and social intelligence (Holmer, 2014).

One other new development has been on the area of mental health, which represents a growing topic. Emerging from more narrow interests around managerial skills such as the ability to manage stress (Adams, 1977) and anxiety (Cohen & Miaoulis, 1978), this literature presents a more holistic focus on overall mental health and well-being through training (Hamdani, 2021), and techniques such as mindfulness (Kuechler & Stedham, 2018). Alongside this focus on mental health has come understanding of the darker side of personalities and how they might adversely play out in organisations. As an example, management education now considers impacts of narcissism in the classroom and how it can be managed (Bergman et al., 2010).

Another area to feature from a Rational School perspective has been the topic of power. As we shall see in the following chapter, while power in the Rational School is not as fundamental as it is in the Critical School, Rational scholars nevertheless consider it an important topic for students to learn. One early example comes from Akin (1979), who details an experiential exercise developed to assist students in understanding French and Raven's (1959) bases of social power – legitimate, expert, referent, reward, punishment, and information. More recent applications include teaching exercises intended to develop a student's social capital (Van Buren & Hood, 2010), simulations designed to provoke student understanding of power in organisations (Kern,

2000), and the use of storytelling for understanding power dynamics (Schor et al., 1996).

Rational scholars differentiate themselves from the Critical School with an understanding of power which suggests potentially positive aspects to authority. Teaching on power in the Rational School therefore includes topics with more optimistic overtones, such as around positive impacts of authority on personality, expertise, control of rewards, and charisma (Bolman & Deal, 2017). This understanding enables wide-ranging discussion on the skills and capabilities of managers and the implications for management education in areas such as coaching (De Haan et al., 2010), where authority has positive connotations in terms of the insight and learning coaches can provide to their clients during critical moments.

To summarise, we can therefore see that tinkerer teachers have embraced teaching of and through technology, as well as the teaching of soft skills, to improve corporate production by building student workplace skills. Discussion on these topics broadly demonstrates that management educators have evolved from an approach of transmitting student skills in areas such as using computer software, to one where technologies and soft skills are increasingly captured in the pedagogies by which students are taught. Hence, the rise of phenomena such as online learning, virtual teams, course agreements, and CAO.

However, Rational scholars also understand that their efforts to improve corporate production through facilitating student skills to become active workplace contributors must take place against an ethical backdrop. Therefore, educators in this school work to assist students in understanding how they should behave in the workplace.

UNDERSTANDING HOW I SHOULD BEHAVE: TEACHING ETHICS IN THE RATIONAL SCHOOL

On the topic of ethics, the overriding intent of the Rational School has again been to mirror skills required by the corporation in meeting its societal obligations, such as through environmental sustainability. Consistent with the evolutionary consequentialist ethics of pragmatism, the Rational School therefore evolves along the way in which corporate responses change to ethical issues. In the 1970s and early 1980s Milton Friedman's maxim that the social responsibility of business was to increase its profits (Friedman, 1970) seems ascendent, however the corporation of today now finds itself at the forefront of responsible management initiatives in transnational bodies such as the United Nations. Following a similar evolution, tinkerer teachers have therefore also chartered a path from a view that they had little role in teaching management ethics, to the rise of a more activist pedagogical approach which shares much in common with a Critical School perspective.

Consistent with this evolution, Rational School debate in the 1980s featured substantive discussion on whether it is fit and proper for the educator to even engage in the teaching of ethics, or whether a hands-off approach is more appropriate. An illustrative example can be found in JME, which features a dispute over whether a professional ethics code is required for bodies representing management educators.

Prompted by Harvard Business School Dean, Derek Bok, who had argued that his institution's curriculum was deficient in business ethics (King, 1983), JME presents a counterpoint debate on the topic in management education. On one side of this debate proponents suggest that a professional code of conduct is established through ethical codes in disciplines such as law and medicine (Yates & Summers, 1986). Arguing that reliance on the law for ethical guidance can only provide a minimal set of standards, the authors put forward their view that management education requires a more advanced position. To support their argument, the authors survey a professional group of educators to understand their views on ethics and ethical issues. Their findings indicate a lack of a common definition on what constitutes ethical behaviour, the suggestion that greater sensitivity is required around potential conflicts of interest, and inconsistent student views on how ethical behaviour from faculty should be demonstrated in their interactions. Yates and Summers conclude that the lack of clarity around such important issues indicates the need for a code of ethics in management education.

In contrast, Jelinek (1986) notes that Yates and Summers' survey does not evidence professorial abuse in the teaching of students, and therefore concludes that a more convincing case for a code of ethics is required. Similarly, the author suggests that as students only engage with a small number of faculty over the time of their studies, there should not be any concern in the survey findings of inconsistent presentation around ethics across the wider profession. Jelinek therefore argues for expanded debate around ethics in management education, noting several topics worthy of discussion including the use of power, self-interest of the professor, notions of a pedagogical 'higher good' (manipulating students to teach them), and the avoidance of appearances of favouritism.

Rising corporate interest in the area soon resolved the topic of ethics as one in which Rational scholars should take interest. First, a series of popular corporate studies emerged which indicated a positive relationship between corporate value systems and success. Prominent was Peters and Waterman's *In Search of Excellence* (1982), an attempt by two McKinsey and Company consultants to identify the secret behind the success of 43 top-performing US companies. Of note was their observation that a key differentiating factor for these companies was their values. Successful organisations were therefore likely to display values-driven leadership, and an associated tight focus on a few core values.

According to the authors, corporate success was driven by leaders capable of articulating a clear set of values and purpose and able to secure the buy-in of employees.

As this emerging focus on values and corporate success came to prominence, a further set of issues brought the topic of ethics into the management education spotlight. Media reporting at the time ensured high public visibility of several corporate activities involving severe detrimental environmental and social impacts. Of note were incidents such as the Bhopal disaster, when nearly 20,000 people died of a poisonous gas release from a pesticide factory (Varma & Varma, 2005), and the Exxon Valdez oil spill which contaminated 1,990 kilometres of pristine Alaskan shoreline and killed hundreds of thousands of seabirds and marine mammals (Peterson et al., 2003). Acid rain, the greenhouse effect, Third World deprivation, depletion of the ozone layer, and wasteful human consumption were all laid at the feet of 'commercial gargantuanism' (Moon, 1989).

A cadre of social groups emerged to provide resistance to adverse corporate activity and redefine expectations of good citizenship in organisations. One prominent case is found in the success of the Greenpeace environmental campaign against Royal Dutch Shell's plans to scrap the Brent Spar oil rig. Having reached the end of its working life, scientists at Shell's UK operations examined options for removing the rig from service. The conclusion from this scientific analysis was that the best environmental and economic solution to the issue would be to sink the rig in the North Sea. Shell scientists argued that such an approach may even have net environmental benefits, their analysis suggesting it was likely that organic and inorganic nutrients from the rig could encourage fish and mollusc species diversity at the dumpsite (Nisbet & Fowler, 1995).

Greenpeace conducted their own environmental assessment and disagreed with Shell's solution, which they concluded was likely to cause environmental degradation of the area. Their response was to leverage a range of activist initiatives for framing Shell across the European continent as a serial polluter and accuse it of planning to pollute again in the future (Bakir, 2006). Consumer boycotts of Shell fuel outlets in Germany were soon replicated across the continent, and the governments of Germany, the Netherlands, Denmark, and Sweden applied pressure on the UK government to revoke their approval of the deep-sea disposal. Greenpeace's actions forced Shell into a retreat on their plans and the company disposed of the rig through other means. For example, parts from the oil rig eventually provided materials for new harbour facilities in Norway. Renowned moral philosopher Alasdair MacIntyre described the Brent Spar incident as a milestone event, where 'a relatively small environmental pressure group won a notable victory over an international industrial giant ...' (1995, p.578).

A rise in anti-corporate activism similar to that of Greenpeace soon forced organisations to take the social conduct of their operations more seriously. Their response was to implement bureaucratic features within their organisational structures by creating roles such as environmental sustainability managers and ethics departments. The Rational School sought to reflect such corporate developments by increasing their emphasis on ethics and environmental sustainability in the management education curriculum.

One pedagogical case which details an emerging acknowledgement of the need for faculty to engage with ethical issues is detailed by McCormick and Fleming (1990). McCormick outlines a story of his teaching in an MBA class. During one lesson, a student spoke up to accuse his employers of falsifying test data around electronic parts for missiles. McCormick reports his shock at the revelation and admits being unsure on how to act ethically in the situation, 'what do I do when a student says, "at my company they are doing something immoral and illegal?"' (McCormick & Fleming, 1990, p.15).

Determined to better understand how he should approach such a conundrum, McCormick engages with a business ethicist, his department chair, and an ethics professor to arrive at an appropriate response. Suggestions from this group lead McCormick to follow up with the student over several in- and out-of-class conversations. McCormick states that despite leveraging personal contacts to verify expected rates of failure for microchips in guidance units, he was unable to resolve whether the microchips were faulty. But he does reflect his satisfaction that by phoning a confidential hotline to report his concerns, the student had taken steps to resolve the issue.

Reflecting on case implications, McCormick and Fleming (1990) suggest that the professor should recognise and define the ethical dilemma, provide support and advice to students who introduce challenging topics, create a caring atmosphere for the whistle-blower by sensitively involving other students in classroom discussions, and seek outside assistance to better understand the ethical dilemma.

JME extend debate on this topic with two pieces in the same issue which engage with ethics of the case. As a precursor to the relativist ethics of the Critical School, Erdynast (1990) turns away from consequentialist notions of ethics, and instead applies Rawls' theory of justice (1971) to the situation. He concludes that McCormick should have engaged in a two-step decision-making procedure: (1) distinguishing between conceptions of the good and conceptions of right and justice; and (2) subordinating concern about classroom issues around student confidentiality to instead recognise that a good is not permissible when an injustice or legal wrong would be required for its attainment.

Meanwhile, Schultheiss (1990), a corporate trainer at the Westinghouse Corporation, puts forward a corporate response to McCormick's ethical dilemma where trainers make allowances for different perceptions, clarify each party's responsibility, understand their limitations in taking on responsibility, understand who their client is (the organisation which is employing them), and consider the long-term effects of any actions.

The original article, and the responses to it, seems to hint at a shift in Rational approaches to ethics. In the first instance, the McCormick case illustrates the shift away from the Rational view of management education as a values-free discipline (Keeley, 1983), and points to subsequent efforts by tinkerers to more explicitly integrate ethics into the business curriculum (e.g. Payne, 1993). However, the response of Erdynast (1990) also advances an ethical perspective beyond that of the corporate response advocated by Schultheiss (1990), suggestive of the more activist post-Millennium approach to scholarship on ethics in management education.

In response to ethical dilemmas facing the corporation, the 1990s period presents a range of innovative pedagogical approaches for integrating ethics into the business curriculum. Some Rational scholars introduce new pedagogies by integrating frameworks such as student ethical codes (Ferris, 1996). Meanwhile, others seek to teach students by incorporating experiential methods such as role-playing activities to learn multi-stakeholder engagement on issues of environment and economy (Egri, 1999) and games for investigating ethics in the control of scarce resources and distribution (Collins, 1999).

This ethics movement raises a central question for the Rational scholar: Is teaching business ethics about developing student skills in ethical issues, or is it about improving their behaviour? Brady (1990) captures a distinction between the management educator as detached intellectual and moral activist. While he settles on the former as a stronger pedagogical and ethical model for the classroom, his motivating question on whether the traditionally detached educator is sufficient for teaching matters of ethics raises the prospect of a more activist approach.

This question is brought into focus at the start of the twenty-first century with the collapse of energy giant Enron. A Texas-based energy, commodities, and services company which claimed revenue of US$101 billion in 2000 (Fortune, 2000), Enron had established a competitive culture where executives sought to maintain explosive growth by creating a false picture of performance through smoke-and-mirrors partnerships and false accounting practices (Sims & Brinkmann, 2003).

Troubling for management educators was that Enron's failure was also founded in a leadership team comprised of MBA graduates from outstanding institutions such as Harvard Business School and the Kellogg School of Management. Scholars concluded that if executives of the top schools had abrogated their ethical responsibilities, then it was indicative that management education had been neglectful of the development of student skills in ethics and had instead pursued an education to encourage 'practically any lengths to increase corporate profits and short-term shareholder return' (Alsop, 2006). A key focus of inquiry became the Rational School itself, which Pfeffer and Fong (2004) accuse of providing an education aimed only at enhancing careers and salaries. In what remains the most-cited piece in the history of AMLE, Ghoshal (2005) goes further in accusing the Rational School of creating a narrow theoretical agenda, ignoring or marginalising questions of ethics and morality, and undermining its scientific empirical basis.

Just when this tumult over the Rational School approach appeared to be fading (Alsop, 2006), ethical concerns returned to the top of the management education agenda with the Global Financial Crisis (GFC). Emerging from a real estate asset bubble and associated financial contagion across many western economies, the subsequent bailouts of investment banks deemed 'too big to fail' (Wright, 2010) prompted further introspection for the Rational School. The question was asked as to why the corporates that had created this situation through dubious financial schemes were the ones to receive government assistance while individuals and families at lower income levels lost their homes and livelihoods. The GFC renewed a push for education which was about more than profitability, and where there would be an emphasis on issues such as sustainability and quality of life (Peoples, 2009). At this time, 'responsible management education' emerges in the literature as a movement which emphasises practical aspects and principles of how to responsibly educate the next generation of management professionals (Forray & Leigh, 2012).

Instigating this approach was the development in 2007 of the United Nations Principles for Responsible Management Education (PRME). The intention of the PRME is to embed sustainability in business education, a 'just and moral obligation of academia' to ensure environmental and social sustainability is fully assimilated across business disciplines (Maloni et al., 2012, p.313). As 'drivers of business behavior', the United Nations believes that academics and universities are necessary to any 'meaningful and lasting change in the conduct of corporations towards societal responsibility and sustainability' (United Nations, 2007, p.3).

The PRME appear to have been met with great enthusiasm by the academic community. By 2015, over 600 higher education institutions across 80 countries had signed up to commitments to responsible management education in areas such as peace, anti-corruption, gender equality, poverty, and environmental sustainability (Forray et al., 2015). Meanwhile, societal impact is now a key commitment required by accreditation programmes such as the Association to Advance Collegiate Schools of Business (AACSB).

For the Rational School, the PRME appears to be indicative of a defining shift in mindset. Rather than simply mirroring the activities of the corporation in pedagogy and curriculum design, management education is now encouraged to step beyond that modelled by markets as a means of inducing responsible corporate behaviour. A leap from moulding student skills to reflect the current demands of the workplace, the notion of responsible management education appears to represent an invitation for a more progressive endeavour. In this approach, the distinction between the Rational School and the Critical School begins to blur. The licence to management educators for greater agency in their curriculum is reflected by consideration of what is 'furthered through our educational endeavors' (Viswanathan, 2012), and involves an 'epistemological shift in pedagogy' (Sroufe et al., 2015).

Associated with this more Critical approach is the move by the Rational School towards a pluralist ethics. If management education is to consider a diverse range of stakeholders and ensure it does not prioritise profit over people, Rational scholars hold the need for a genuinely pluralistic view of principles which does not assign absolute order or provide a single unifying theme (Burton et al., 2006). Therefore, where management education might once have coalesced around western ideals such as Christian spirituality, minority traditions are now integrated into classroom practice. For example, Pielstick (2005) introduces the idea of spiritual synchronicity, which brings religious practices, objects, holidays, and values from different parts of the world to his management education classroom.

For the Rational School, the more activist approach to education implicated by the PRME and pluralist positions represents a shift which would have likely been unthinkable to the authors of the Ford and Carnegie reports. The position is reflected by AMLE, where the management education agenda now unambiguously puts forward an activist model: 'it is time to use our position and influence to have an impact on the future of academic values, management and organizational norms, and institutions' (Greenberg & Hibbert, 2022, p.164). Over time, we can therefore see an evolution on the topic of ethics in the Rational School from the management educator as detached observer, to one where the tinkerer is expected to advance through their classroom practice student skills and capabilities that target a greater social good.

EMBRACING EQUALITY: NAVIGATING RACIAL AND SEXUAL IDENTITY IN THE WORKPLACE

For the Rational School, the issue of identity in management education shows a similar trajectory to that of ethics. Where scholars might once have overlooked or remained relatively muted on topics related to individual identity, the current literature is now common with exploration of topics in this area. This development includes the evolution from a pedagogy in the 1970s and 1980s that reflects the need for mainly white male students to improve their skills in managing organisational diversity and equality, to one targeted at a range of potential managers on matters of equity which include race, sex, and sexual identity.

In the 1970s, identity issues seem only rarely discussed. Coverage during this time is mainly targeted at the level of structural changes in the classroom, such as an observed increase in the number of female and minority students (Strauss, 1977), or aimed at better preparing white male managers for working with women and minorities (Seashore, 1976). By the late 1970s, the increasingly diverse nature of the US workforce meant the need for development programmes to include teaching around racism and sexism in their curriculum. Again, this new agenda was often directed at improving the skills of white male managers, with benefits set out in terms of how better management of a diverse workforce might assist the organisation to improve its productivity, meet its legal obligations, and address ethical and social concerns (Brown, 1979).

The early 1980s saw a rise in the number of courses directed at management development opportunities for women. Where Rational management education may once have argued negligible differences between men and women in the workforce, proponents of these new courses held that women in management experienced problems in ways that were qualitatively different from men (Cunningham, 1981). Pedler (1981) takes the opportunity to detail awkward male to female exchanges in management development settings from his attendance at a conference comprising a mixed group discussion on issues of sex in the workplace. Detailing awkward feelings of 'fancying' a female participant from afar, to the 'uneasy' sensation of noting the supportive demeanour of females in the group when finding out each other's names or checking for feelings of apprehension, Pedler sets out a case for balancing the 'awful manliness of our organisations' (1981, p.18).

Accompanying this notion that there might be different challenges for men and women in the workplace came discussion on other sexual domains and how they might play out in the organisation. Mezoff (1983) presents a pioneering approach for assisting management educators to confront issues of gay and lesbian workforce discrimination. Recognising 20 million Americans as having a homosexual orientation, Mezoff introduces a pedagogical approach for teaching about gay and lesbian discrimination by using a film called *Word Is Out* (Adair et al., 1977) to prompt discussion on homosexual stereotypes.

Based on interviews with 26 people speaking about their experiences of being gay and lesbian, the author appears to herald a distinction between earlier morally neutral approaches to topics of identity and more advanced contemporary positions on the issue. Mezoff says, 'it's important to deal with the issue as a managerial issue and not a moral one. Neither our MBAs nor anyone else likes being preached to' (1983, p.32). However, he also provides an afterword to the piece which hints at the coming shift in perception on the responsibilities of the management education teacher. He concludes, 'OB teachers have some important advantages in their attempts to influence their MBA students on issues of social discrimination: students are a captive audience; professors have high position power; and this activity [on sexual identity discrimination] fits the teacher's legitimate role of provoking and stimulating students' (Mezoff, 1983, p.33).

In the mid-1980s also came an emerging recognition of the potential for women to assume managerial positions in organisations. Concern at women's lack of progress into management became a theme in the management education literature (Hammond & Boydell, 1985). In response, business schools began offering courses on Women in Management. This development raised several questions for faculty, such as whether men should be allowed to undertake such studies and whether a male could teach such a course (Hai, 1982).

Offering insights on their own experiences on excluding/including a cohort of men from undertaking Women in Management courses, Spelman and colleagues (1986) consider whether men should be allowed to participate in such educational opportunities. Identifying the benefits of raising consciousness in men of the workplace challenges confronting women, versus men's feelings of frustration and anger in confronting this changing world, the authors conclude that it is worthwhile to include men in Women in Management courses.

However, settling debate on whether it was appropriate for these courses to be taught by male faculty proved more difficult. Bartolome presents an essay on his experience of teaching women about women, including a cohort he feels 'sound angry and extremely unhappy about living in what they see as a male dominated world', and whom he thinks 'have been actively involved in the women's liberation movement and are committed to it' (1990, p.47). While expressing the view that many women enjoy his classes, Bartolome concludes that he is in a 'no-win situation' in Women in Management classes, and that he will 'have to learn to live with the fact that a minority of women will react negatively to me when, in my teaching, I address the female experience' (1990, p.51).

Management educators in the 1980s also began to appreciate the prospect that people of colour might become managers. Here, the work of Waters is important in bringing into the management education literature perspectives from outside the field which indicate that 'minority managers do face a host of problems that are unique to them', and that 'there is a great need on the part of minority students to be prepared to function effectively in their working environment' (1989, p.38). As we shall see, discussion on issues of interracial workplaces again rose to prominence in the mid-1990s.

Similar to the corporate incidents which had driven the push in the 1980s for a greater focus on ethics in management education, macro-environment events in the 1990s also served to push increased workforce diversity and interest in how they should be managed. One prominent development was increased corporate globalisation, driven by developments in technology which enabled greater reach in business communication and logistics. Corporate behemoths such as Microsoft and Coca-Cola provided pointers to an emerging globalised reality for many western corporations of diverse workforces, and complex issues in structural or cultural change (Malekzadeh, 1998). This development required Rational scholars to cultivate student skills in cross-cultural competence and encouraged a range of educational activities for ensuring that the western manager could competently manage a foreign workforce (Bartz et al., 1990). Meanwhile, other pedagogical activities were intended to provide people from developing and undeveloped countries with skill sets for becoming competent managers (Ronan, 1993).

Issues of race returned to the fore following the beating of Black man Rodney King by Los Angeles police officers in 1991. But it was the 1995 trial and subsequent acquittal of African American football player, O.J. Simpson, on charges of murdering his white former wife and her friend, which created what has been described as an 'intellectual riot' between Black and white employees across the United States (*Wall Street Journal*, 1995). The incident provided an opportunity for Powell and Taylor (1998), a white professor and a Black student in an MBA diversity course, to outline a pedagogical technique for better teaching students to navigate racial issues. Through using a skit, the authors show three different ways workplace conversations between a white and a Black employee on the O.J. Simpson trial verdict might play out. The first presents a negative encounter in which racial prejudices are displayed, the second details what happens when conversation avoids racial issues, and the third presents what the authors suggest is a positive discussion, where racial stereotypes are avoided.

Confronting discrimination against homosexual members of the workforce also made its way more explicitly as a topic into the management curriculum at this time. Gay and lesbian workers initially represented a complex organisational phenomenon because contrary to workers with physically differentiating features of sex, race, and disability, sexual orientation can be hidden from colleagues. Preventing discrimination against homosexual workers would therefore mean equipping students for dealing sensitively with a population which may not be visibly apparent.

To this end, McQuarrie (1998), leverages a case study on a man who has HIV and whom fellow workers are demanding be fired. The case plays out through two different scenarios. In the first iteration, the man is in a heterosexual marriage, provides sole support for his family, and has acquired HIV through a blood transfusion. In the second version, the man is single and is only able to provide for himself through the job, but he is gay and has acquired the virus through a homosexual relationship. Analysis of student reactions to the case suggest that those engaging with the heterosexual case were focused on protecting the man's rights and educating his co-workers, while those in the homosexual case were more interested in isolating, segregating, or relocating him. McQuarrie suggests the results indicate the need to introduce sexual orientation as a topic in management courses, as well as introduce non-discriminatory terms such as 'partner' for describing spouses (1998, p.170).

Management education also turned attention to other workplace topics which had once been considered taboo. Surveys showing that 40 per cent of females had encountered sexual harassment in the workplace meant educators sought new ways to develop student skills in examining issues such as links between sexual harassment and power, gender differences in career advancement, gender relations in the workplace, and organisational responses to sexual harassment (Comer & Cooper, 1998). For Rational scholars, the rationale behind integrating such topics into management education has always been put as being about breaking down barriers and working towards equality (Jackson, 2005).

However, the post-Millennium period appears to have disrupted this narrative. Finding articles on identity from this period which can be considered genuinely Rational is a challenging endeavour. An early pointer to the difficulties of the Rational School in taking an equality approach to issues of identity is summarised by Sikula (1995) with a focus on differences between ethnic and ethic diversity. Taking ethnic diversity as a push for integration, where organisations focus on creating conditions for human rights, equal opportunity, and non-discrimination, the author argues that corporations instead often implement ethic diversity, where affirming a specific group creates 'diversity, difference, and divisiveness' (Sikula, 1995, p.257).

The Sikula article is important for representing a fork in the road for the Rational School, where identity scholarship now seems to blur with that of the Critical School in trending towards equity over equality. One example can be found in Verbos and colleagues' (2011) 'Coyote Was Walking ...'. The paper attempts to deconstruct traditional western notions of time by introducing temporal constructs from a Native American perspective but would appear equally at home in either school. For the Rational scholar, the paper likely represents an important part of normalising the Native American Indian segment of the corporate workforce, while its appeal for the Critical Scholar would appear to be on taking the perspective of a marginalised group for upending a previously taken-for-granted and powerful social construction.

To manage this small-c critical turn in the classroom, Rational pedagogies have also adopted more distinctively constructivist techniques around language games which appear more consistent with Critical perspectives. For example, Gherardi and Murgia (2015) require students to complete a short story in which they imagine giving feedback to a female or a male boss. Analysis of these narratives shows a declining image of the male manager, and a construct of care around what constitutes good management for both male and female CEOs. Such pedagogical techniques suggest a Rational scholarship in identity which now appears to embrace a turn towards equity.

CONCLUSION

Reflecting on the evolution of the Rational School, we can see several key developments over the past 50 years. It is noteworthy that the Rational School appears to have been at the core of management education in the twentieth century. Early efforts by management educators to build their own and the field's legitimacy were founded in the development of the Rational School. Hence, efforts by Gordon and Howell (1959) and Pierson (1959) to embrace the liberal and treat management education as aligning to an American national project of building student skills for use in industry.

At the heart of this world is an American pragmatism, less philosophical in nature, and more attuned to an 'effectiveness in action' (Joullie & Spillane, 2020, p.257). On this basis, the aim of a manager is to take actions which will achieve results for the organisation's shareholders, and the goal of management education is therefore about the efforts of the teacher in building key workplace skills for the students.

The post-1970 journey of Rational scholarship has been dedicated to several issues. In terms of the types of skills organisations require, there was an initial divergence between management education which focused on soft skills such as communication and motivation (e.g. Jenster & Duncan, 1987), and hard skills involved with technology, analysis, and decision making (e.g. Solomon, 1979). However, the mid-1990s development of the internet appears to have done much to dissolve this distinction. The information superhighway enables virtual learning through new multimedia and classroom tools (Bilimoria, 1999). This technology has evolved to include developments such as social media (Lim et al., 2014), where distinctions between hard and soft skills now blur to the extent that individuals can be both content creators and consumers. The COVID-19 pandemic and the associated rush to online learning means technology has become a near ubiquitous feature of the modern management education environment, a feature likely to be accelerated by the Fourth Industrial Revolution and its promise of mass personalised learning (Fukami et al., 2022).

In terms of ethics, the journey of the Rational School has been from one of the teacher as neutral and detached observer (Brady, 1990), to one where ethics occupies a central role in present-day education. From the mid-1980s debate over whether a management education code of conduct was required

(Yates & Summers, 1986; Jelinek, 1986), issues such as McCormick's conundrum on how to act on his student's report of failed test data on missile parts (McCormick & Fleming, 1990) have driven a more concerted effort to explicitly incorporate ethics into the curriculum. The collapse of Enron and Arthur Andersen at the turn of the Millennium and the subsequent Global Financial Crisis have then driven critique against the Rational School that it marginalises issues of morality (Ghoshal, 2005). The associated development of the United Nations PRME (2007) and subsequent adoption by business schools has seen goals of social, environmental, and economic sustainable development occupy a position at the heart of management education (Audebrand & Pepin, 2022).

Noteworthy in this development has been a growing indistinction between Rational and Critical approaches to ethics. Consistent with Dewey's (1922) view of ethics as an evolving consequentialism based on the expression of free will and the practical results of action, as workplaces become more racially diverse and focused on environmentally sustainable goals the Rational School appears to be devolving towards a more pluralist ethics (Burton et al., 2006). While the 1970s featured scholarship intended to help white males to manage women and racial minorities in the workforce (e.g. Seashore, 1976), and the 1980s featured efforts to boost women into leadership positions in organisations (e.g. Hai, 1982), since the mid-1990s there have been more concerted efforts to focus on racial and sexual minorities in the workforce. Therefore, we see the development of pedagogies such as skits on racially charged issues such as the O.J. Simpson trial (Powell & Taylor, 1998), or issues painted by authors as associated with sexual minorities, such as employees with HIV (McQuarrie, 1998).

With the evolution away from consequentialist and towards pluralist ethical approaches, the Rational School takes an approach to the individual which appears to be moving away from an embrace of equality and more towards pedagogy based on equity. Such an approach is more consistent with the Critical School, as featured in the next chapter.

QUESTIONS FOR THE READER

1. Quickly write down your three immediate takes on the foundations of the Rational School. Do these foundations match your own beliefs and values on management education?
2. The pragmatic beliefs at the heart of the Rational School do not quite appear aligned with the push by Gordon and Howell (1959) and Pierson (1959) to increase the legitimacy of the field and its professionals through scientific empiricism. Do you think a greater empirical basis for management education would better achieve this objective?

3. Do you consider yourself to be focused on teaching either soft or hard skills? To what extent is the other implicated in the teaching of your preferred skill set? (I.e. if you consider yourself as a teacher of soft skills, to what extent are hard skills involved?)
4. What have been the key outcomes from the ethical shift in the Rational School away from teachers as detached intellectuals and towards social activists? Do you believe the profession loses or gains in this shift?
5. What would you do if, like McCormick & Fleming (1990), a student raised ethical concerns about the practices of their workplace? Write down a five-point action plan based on issues such as where you would seek advice, how you would reach an appropriate course of action, and how you would communicate with relevant stakeholders.
6. 'To overcome a lack of effective teaching materials I've collected a number of resources for teaching about gay/lesbian discrimination' (Mezoff, 1983, p.31). Think of a key issue today where you believe there are a lack of effective teaching materials in preparing students for the workplace. What types of resources would you collect to address this issue? Think of key cultural resources (movies, podcasts, newspaper articles, etc.) you might curate to provide instruction on this matter. Devise a lesson plan based on these materials.

4. A brief (and incomplete) history of the Critical School

The rebel teacher stared at the textbook. It was yet another insult, dedicated to perpetuating a worldview of the organisation as a benign force for good. Worse still, it stripped organisations of their colour. You didn't have to be around any organisation for more than about two seconds to realise they were a hotbed of swirling emotions, motivations, and contested terrains. What was set out before the students on the page was a typically lifeless affair, platitudes from some pale, male corporate CEO speaking about how his vision had made his organisation great again, with backup from the Chief Financial Officer who had seen sales rise 450 per cent, and one small paragraph on how they'd introduced recyclable packaging as their commitment to a greener planet. The final assignment in the course was on strategy implementation. This was the best the textbook could put forward? In the educator's opinion, business cases didn't ever really pick up on the complexities and nuances of strategy implementation in organisations. They only told one side of a story and never really grasped the politics which could be at play behind the scenes. And they were boring. Words on a paper which rarely seemed to capture the excitement and intensity of what really happens in an organisation. Where was the janitor who had been underpaid for the last five years but didn't dare speak up for fear of losing her job? Where was the secretary who suffered routine harassment from the CEO and only stayed on because she had three kids to support and an unemployed husband? Where was the Accounts Payable Manager who had missed out on the Chief Financial Officer's job because 23 years of graft in the organisation had gone unrecognised? The rebel teacher closed the textbook, turned to their computer, and began to type.

INTRODUCTION

In terms of a metaphor, the image of the educator in the Critical School is that of a rebel, similar to Luke Skywalker and Princess Leia from the *Star Wars* movies (Lucas, 1977). At its essence, *Star Wars* has been called a space opera, a genre in which the universe is in peril. The original film follows the adventures of key characters Skywalker and Leia as they lead a ragtag rebel force to victory against a tyrannical empire (Star Wars Ventures, 1977; Gordon, 1978).

Similar to *Star Wars*, the Critical School of management education provides the story of a world in peril (Ghoshal, 2005) from a dark empire of neoliberalism (Fotaki & Prasad, 2015), and an educator who must come to its rescue (Greenberg & Hibbert, 2022). Overt links in *Star Wars* between the villainous Darth Vader and Nazism as characterised by his helmet and the uniform of his guards (Gordon, 1978) are also reminiscent of the Critical School's founding crusade against Nazism and Fascism.

In Skywalker, we can see a young man who must overthrow the shadow of his father (Vader), similar again to the Critical School's campaign against traditional institutions such as the family (Del Noce & Lancellotti, 2015). In Princess Leia we see a feminist hero, smart, funny, and unafraid to talk back to the authority of Vader (Mizejewski et al., 2021), similar to the Critical School's emphasis on hearing oppressed and marginalised voices.

Since the turn of the Millennium, the Critical School seems to represent the dominant published approach to management education. While *Management Learning* (ML) had always been a bastion of Critical thought, *Journal of Management Education* (JME) and the newly arrived *Academy of Management Learning and Education* (AMLE) started to take a Critical twist following the corporate scandals at Enron and Arthur Andersen in the early 2000s. The rise of this school in management education scholarship is a notable story in the post-Millennium period. Here, we investigate the world of the Critical School and its impact on management education.

CRITICAL SCHOOL FOUNDATIONS

The world of the Critical School is based on foundations of opposition to the totalitarian, a philosophy of radical poststructuralism, an ethics of moral relativism, and a view of authority as freedom from. These foundations are set out in Figure 4.1.

The Critical School is motivated by a hardened opposition to Fascism. Its historical basis is in philosophers of the Frankfurt School, whose great challenge in the 1920s was in distancing itself from Nazism and Fascism, a project reflected by key Frankfurt School thinkers such as Herbert Marcuse (1968) and Erich Fromm (1941). Such philosophers have engaged with the idea of freedom, a response to what they see as a suppression of individuality in society and a prevailing democratic unfreedom (Marcuse, 1964). Where authority in the Rational School had meant a 'freedom to' through the author-itativeness of figures such as the manager (Spillane & Joullie, 2021), for the Critical School views on authority are of a 'freedom from' to be actively resisted and overcome (Del Noce & Lancellotti, 2015). Critical pedagogy therefore takes a negative view of authority and aims for student emancipation from traditional institutional structures.

The sense of how the concept of freedom should apply in education has most actively been pursued by Brazilian educator Paulo Freire. Recognised as the founder of Critical pedagogy, Freire established education as a battle between the oppressed and oppressors. In this conflict, the key educational task is to enable the oppressed to gain a sense of humanity. Freire perceives educa-

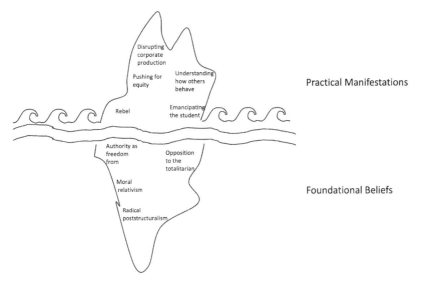

Figure 4.1   The world of the Critical School

tion as a 'practice of freedom'. He sets up this argument by quoting Fromm's earlier work on freedom, and the view that man [*sic*] 'conforms to anonymous authorities and adopts a self which is not his [*sic*] … In spite of a veneer of optimism and initiative, modern man [*sic*] is overcome by a profound feeling of powerlessness which makes him gaze toward approaching catastrophes as though he were paralyzed' (Fromm, 1960, pp.255–256).

For Freire, what society requires is people capable of a flexible, critical spirit for perceiving its contradictions. Identifying and exploring such contradictions will progress the transition away from reactionary forces which maintain power structures of the status quo and prompt the establishment of a new progressive society where humans can rise above those who attempt to silence them. According to Freire, this radical position is:

> a positive stance. The man who has made a radical option does not deny another man's right to choose, nor does he try to impose his own choice … The radical does, however, have the duty imposed by love itself to react against the violence of those who try to silence him – of those who, in the name of freedom, kill his freedom and their own. (Freire, 2021, p.9)

Education is essential to Freire's project as it distinguishes elements belonging to the new order and enables people's critical consciousness by encouraging them to reflect on 'themselves, their responsibilities, and their role in the new cultural climate' (Freire, 2021, p.13).

A seminal event in the development of the Critical School is the French student revolts of 1968, a series of protests where students attacked the university system for creating an enforced conformity whose production of knowledge had been used for the purposes of power and domination (Best & Kellner, 1991). Critical educators maintain the spirit of this revolution by aiming to emancipate the student from oppressive structures. This agenda means enabling members of society to 'alter their lives by fostering in them the sort of self-knowledge and understanding of their social conditions which can serve as the basis for such an alteration' (Fay, 1987, p.23).

The Critical perspective remained an outlier in much of early management education thought. Its rise to prominence began in the 1980s, when opposition to the neoliberal economic reforms of Ronald Reagan and Margaret Thatcher prompted scholars to seek alternatives (Fox, 2009). One source of inspiration for scholars opposing the neoliberal agenda was to be found in the thoughts of Freire, prompting the rise of an emerging group of scholars seeking to prioritise societal goals and counter free market zealotry (Snell, 1989).

French philosopher Michel Foucault (1977) also came to prominence at this time for his views on society as consisting of power structures in which people were subjugated into an existence of control and dependence. The challenge for the rebel teacher is therefore to emancipate students from power structures they may not be able to see and which they take for granted. The postmodern position associated with Foucault and his understanding of the world as infinitely subjective places it at odds with the Rational School and its basis in rational knowledge. For the Critical scholar, not only can there be no such objective basis of knowledge, but any rhetoric, authority, or tradition which underlines such thinking should be marked by scepticism and resistance (Mingers, 2000).

Chief among those institutions from which the Critical management education scholar seeks to emancipate the student are engines of the neoliberal economy: the organisation; the manager; and the business school itself. The organisation is seen as a repressive western capitalist endeavour, exploitative of those living in poverty, and uncommitted to distributive justice (Collins, 1996). In contrast to the Rational School and its perceptions of the organisation as a force for good, Critical scholars occasionally perceive the organisation as stupid and absurd (Azevedo, 2023), but more frequently as a neoliberal enterprise which penetrates into most aspects of our lives through an 'I' perspective on economic action which subsumes moral sentiments (Shah et al., 2022).

Critical studies also reveal managers as a privileged social group, rising to power through historical processes which appear universal and inevitable (Willmott, 2012), and entrenching 'thought and activity which is being used to justify considerable cruelty and inequality' (Parker, 2002, p.9).

By extension of the critique on organisations, business schools and management education are considered by Critical scholars as western hegemonic forces to resist (Neal & Finlay, 2008). For example, Liu (2022) presents the view that while management education has promoted capitalism as an inevitable and ideal way of life, it is based on a structural and cultural whiteness which is often invisible to its participants. Critical scholars therefore perceive Rational School management education teachers as engaging in an immoral endeavour of training students to perform successfully in the workplace. An early piece by Garratt sums up this view, where he laments that 'management schools [have] got their heads down to work for the scientists and industrialists who [are] literally killing them' (1972, p.4). Meanwhile, management theory taught in business schools by the Rational School is perceived as 'an expression of technocratic thinking that seeks to manipulate human potential and desire in order to bolster a falsely naturalized status quo' (Alvesson & Willmott, 1992, p.436).

The rebel teacher therefore perceives their job as being to disrupt the pipeline of corporate production, an endeavour which includes resisting the corporate university, and establishes an attitude towards academics as 'sycophantic servants to multinational business' (Jones et al., 2020, p.365). Critical scholars argue that the Rational production line perspective to management education is based on white males unethically imposing themselves over others and ignoring any accountability to a wider set of values:

> a system [which] teaches white, middle-class men to believe that we are right ... We are led to believe that the world will fall apart unless we hold ourselves together. If we are to be strong and responsible, it is necessary for us to believe in our own rightness and our own rights. (Vince, 1990, p.51)

Behind the Critical School lies an ethics of moral relativism. Railing against the western ethnocentrism they see as comprising the modernist period, Critical scholars focus on liberating students from a European and American monopoly on values and beliefs by enabling the rise of different cultural traditions for reflecting and interpreting human experience (Fox & Moult, 1990). The moral relativist position is founded in the rights perspective associated with US ethicist, John Rawls. The rights movement perceives the need to overcome social injustice and constraints on personal freedom (White & Taft, 2004). To meet this intent, the rights approach establishes universal principles of human rights, within which individuals have moral autonomy. This means equal basic liberties for all, but with an established principle of difference where social and economic inequalities are to be arranged so they can be of greatest benefit to the least-advantaged members of society (Messerly, 2015).

This ethics of moral relativism therefore places an emphasis on the other, elevating the social rights of society's marginalised and oppressed. Based on interpretive empirical foundations, the Critical School opposes positive Rational ontologies, instead offering relational and Indigenous ways of knowing as subjective understandings of the world. The rebel teacher of the Critical School therefore seeks to elevate racial and sexual minorities over more established forms of authority.

For Critical scholars this ethical framework means upending 'pale, male and stale' views on management (McLaren et al., 2021), and championing marginalised groups such as the Global South (Wanderley et al., 2021) and minority racial communities (Prieto et al., 2021). Importantly, the moral relativism of the Critical approach also means reflexivity is paramount. Reflexivity is about critically probing one's own beliefs and assumptions for addressing how their own identity leads them to be attuned to certain phenomena rather than others (McDonald, 2016). How management educators teach, research, and engage with others will therefore be driven by an individual's identity.

Laasch and colleagues (2022a) identify several ontologies associated with the Critical School. Grouped under broad umbrellas of Critical and poststructural ontologies, these include Critical historical, Indigenous, process, relational, site, performativity, and post-humanist ontologies. Consistent across these ontologies is the belief that there is no fixed reality. Subjectivist realities are to be found in historical power structures (Critical historical ontology), varieties of local cosmologies (Indigenous ontology), processes (process ontology), relations (relational ontology), local social sites (site ontology), enactment of social realities (performativity), and entanglement between human and non-human actors (post-humanist ontologies).

The radical nature of the Critical School means practitioners often balance the more utopian demands of a wider Critical emancipation (Large-C Critical) with that of a more incremental project (small-c critical). This challenge is illustrated by Wallo et al. (2022) as one of a critique for improvement versus a critique for emancipation. According to this perspective, critique for improvement uses critical reflection aimed at changing organisational practices, while critique for emancipation aims at freedom from repressive ideological and social conditions found in institutions such as the organisation itself. Therefore, we can see a tension in management education between learning which looks to improvement by transforming taken-for-granted socio-political organisational routines and practices (Jarzabkowski & Whittington, 2008a), versus that which presents a 'harsh dismissal' of mainstream management literature (Wallo et al., 2022) and engages more explicitly with theories around gender and ethnicity to provoke management educators to join wider social movements such as Black Lives Matter (Edmondson et al., 2020).

The result of this flight from authority is a Critical pedagogy which sets itself against Rational empirical methods to establish interpretive techniques for exploring issues in six main areas: rhetoric, tradition, power, objectivity, reflexivity, and reality (Rosile & Boje, 1996). To undertake this mission, the school is established in a pluralist ethics which aims to enable marginalised and oppressed minority groups. Rebel teachers lead the way in moving beyond notions of equality to engage in principles of equity for emancipating those marginalised by their racial and sexual identities.

The Critical perspective in management education is established by Pugh's opening edition editorial for ML which states, 'management teachers can exert a strong and beneficial influence on the future of such [management] education' (1970, p.1). However, where rebel teachers may once have comprised a niche area of scholarship, the Critical School of today is arguably the dominant approach in management education. As we shall see, management education now regularly features topics on diversity and ethics taken from a more radical perspective. The following therefore offers an introduction to what appears to be the prevailing school in management education.

DISRUPTING CORPORATE PRODUCTION

When it comes to disrupting corporate production, the Critical School establishes pedagogical techniques which seek to emancipate students from traditional sources of western authority. Central to this endeavour has been to provide an understanding of how power structures work through teaching political skills. Combined with this educational endeavour has come a focus on instilling in students a capacity for resisting authority. This ambition often plays out through linguistic techniques for uncovering systems of marginalisation and oppression which may otherwise remain invisible. As we shall see, efforts to disrupt corporate production also imply a more activist role for the rebel teacher.

Essential to the Critical School is the notion of power. Critical scholars perceive power structures as pervasive and coercive (Ferdinand, 2004). Their ambition is therefore to uncover and disintegrate power structures within the organisation and wider society. Central to this endeavour has been ML, the field's leading Critical journal, where Scott provides an early take on power as a system to be escaped. Scott (1972, p.114) takes a view of life as 'an experience which no-one would wish upon himself [*sic*] if he [*sic*] had the choice', and consistent with Fromm's views on authority he argues the main endeavour for improving one's own existence should be to achieve a subjective freedom from forces outside of oneself by understanding how power structures impose personal deference.

While early work in management education rarely engaged with the concept of power explicitly, the concept remains implicit in several works. Included in this is a focus on the notion of alienation. Lessam (1974) examines how the capitalist production system alienates workers from the product of their labour. The author argues that functions of the organisation including production management, marketing, finance, and personnel management provide fertile ground for worker alienation. Betraying the Critical School's societal concerns, Lessam points to demands from government and the public for business to become more socially responsible. He also provides an early pointer to Critical School philosophy on the role of critical reflection by maintaining that change in the business context will be driven by 'an awakening of individual awareness, responsibility and concern' (1974, p.18). Similar early attempts to focus on marginalised and alienated parties are explored through a focus on the unemployed (Huczynski, 1978) and managers at retirement (Harrison, 1973).

Given Rational School links between management education and the neoliberal capitalist system of production to which Critical scholars are opposed, rebel educators soon established management education itself as consisting of underlying power structures which were detrimental to the individual and their freedom. One prominent early critique centred on the power of the management educator. Where the Rational School establishes a model of the teacher as a neutral observer, Critical scholars rebuke such a stance. Handy presents a critique of the Rational model as 'merely replicating the ways of the present in the men and women of the future', by educating students to meet marketplace fashions. His view is that educators should 'ignore the pendulum of fashion', and 'stick to unpopular beliefs, particularly in the face of a fashionable consensus' (Handy, 1977, p.59). Early Critical scholars in management education therefore present the possibility of a more 'proactive role' for management schools in being 'a responsible partner in the construction ... of future advanced societies' (Talpaert, 1978, p.149).

Implicit in this critique of the educator was to expose prevailing Rational School pedagogies, such as the Louis Allen approach for developing organisational leaders. Critical scholars saw such a technique as seeking to establish a common vocabulary and philosophy of manager development, a development they opposed on grounds of 'indoctrination' and 'dogma' (Henderson, 1973, p.34).

While early 1970s works hinted at the notion of power, by the late 1970s scholarship began to consider the topic more explicitly. At first, this discussion took place through book reviews which surveyed works on power in scholarship outside of management education. In a review of Martin's *The Sociology of Power* (1977), Whitley (1977) leverages the author's discussion on labour exploitation in systems of slavery, feudalism, and capitalism to introduce readers to emerging notions of power as a subjective force which resides in the structure of specific social relations. Wickens (1979) provides a review on *The Craft of Power* by former US Army scientist turned management consultant Ralph Siu (1979). Wickens claims that Siu presents as a Machiavellian manager, where moral judgement is only used to the extent of its instrumentality, where a checklist of 'weaponry' for the budding executive is presented to assist them in becoming persons of power (Wickens, 1979).

One of the first original management education works on power is provided by Chandler (1979), who portrays the manager as a 'political animal'. However, distinct from the Critical School's negative take on power, Chandler leaves open the possibility that there can be positive and moral aspects to the manager's use of authority. He illustrates good managers as leading through consent rather than authority, demonstrating effective communication, and remaining sympathetic to the aspirations of their workers. Soon, management educators began to contemplate how they might teach students in the art of political skill. Baddeley and James (1987) introduce a 2 x 2 matrix of political skill based on animal metaphors, representing actors as politically inept (donkey), innocent (sheep), clever (fox), or wise (owl). Their ambition with these metaphors is to guide students towards skills complementing a wise organisational actor who is both politically aware and acts with integrity.

By the late 1980s, Critical scholars began to introduce the idea that not only was power a pervasive feature of organisations, but also that it could be invisible to participants. Integral to the Critical position is a view that traditions inherent to western institutions such as the church or the state bring a range of assumptions and attitudes which often establish boundaries on debates and challenges (Mingers, 2000). Similarly, the Critical School is suspicious of the limits to progress presented by power structures of the organisation.

In this vein, Tosey (1989) introduces the notion of unconscious dynamics to make the case that organisations have a dark side. Such work appears important in paving the way for more critical understandings of power to emerge in the post-Millennium period, including studies which prosecute the case that management education is itself an example of a hidden power structure. Such viewpoints result in the perspective that cultural elements such as managerial discourse represent hidden power structures which silence the voice of students (Hjorth, 2003).

For rebel teachers, uncovering these hidden power structures is made possible through techniques of linguistic analysis. Postmodern philosopher Jacques Derrida claims 'there is no outside-text', meaning that the world itself is built on language where words can only find their meaning in relation to other words, and where there can be no closure of knowledge but instead an endless variety of contradictions, unconscious writings, and temporary meanings (Joullie & Spillane, 2020).

The linguistic turn was accelerated in the 1980s by the emerging perspective in the wider field of organisation studies that the world had entered the postmodern era. This shift upends philosophies attached to the Rational School with its basis based on objective knowledge, and establishes a view of the world in which knowledge is constructed through subjective meanings and interpretations (Smircich & Stubbart, 1985). With its subjective basis and endeavour to undermine objective understandings of knowledge, the postmodern understanding complements the Critical School approach. The development also appears to have provided impetus for the Critical School to express its views more explicitly on the topic of power.

An important marker in this development is to be found in Owen's (1983) piece on a public inquiry into a mining accident which killed five men in South Yorkshire in 1975. Moving beyond the sometimes-positive aspects of power championed by Chandler (1979), Owen adopts a negative understanding of authority inspired by German sociologist, Max Weber. In leveraging Weber's main questions on obedience, 'when and why do men [sic] obey?', and 'upon what inner justifications and upon what external means does domination rest?', Owen provides a piece which illustrates authority as a phenomenon from which to flee (1983, p.114).

Owen is motivated in his study by the behaviour at the testimonial inquiry on the accident of surviving miner, Roy Buckley. Owen is intrigued that Buckley's evidence had presented him as a man committed to individual thought, and yet his actions during the accident presented him as a rule follower. Buckley testified that he had undertaken extensive individual research on mining methods, as a result of which he had formed an unfavourable opinion on the knowledge and abilities of junior mine site officials. During his testimony, Buckley also demonstrated that he was not awed by those in authority; he remained critical of the National Coal Board of Management for failing to inform his wife of the accident and subsequent rescue.

In the mine explosion, the team leader had been killed. The puzzle for Owen was that when there was a dispute between co-workers about the best way to escape the pit, Buckley had rather meekly followed the command of the deputy leader, 'this is the way we're going, I am the deputy' (Owen, 1983, p.115). Here was Buckley, seemingly not afraid of authority and with misgivings on the quality of his leaders, who in a life-or-death situation had blindly followed a leader for whom he maintained little respect. Returning to the Weberian understanding of sources of authority in traditional, charismatic, and rational legitimacies (1968), Owen concludes that Buckley's decision to obey is contingent on nothing other than a rational-legal form of authority inherent to the deputy's position. Without the power of the positional title, Owen suggests Buckley's decision would likely have been different.

Soon, critical reflexive studies on power were published in which individuals critiqued their own bases of authority. One prominent example can be found in Nixon's (1986) essay on power and patterns in people and organisations. An executive within the Sun Alliance Insurance Group in the UK, the author presents an introspective take on his own managerial experience, noting his capacity for acting inappropriately in certain situations, and deficiencies in his character.

By the 1990s, claims of a new postmodern management were becoming more established (Carter & Jackson, 1990), giving rise to linguistic techniques for exposing power structures. Famed organisations such as Disney were now portrayed in the wider organisation studies literature as storytelling vehicles, whose purpose was to pursue a heroic official account of themselves and marginalise or repress all voices which chose to present different accounts (Boje, 1995).

The postmodern linguistic turn provoked occasional spot-fires of debate between Critical postmodernists seeking to bring about a new order, and Rationalists looking to reassert their once-prevailing positions on objectivity and rationality. Barry and Elmes (1997) followed up the Boje piece by putting forward the notion of organisational strategy as a story, a rhetorical fiction created by senior leaders to persuade others towards certain understandings and actions. This take was rejected by Rational scholars, who acknowledged that a narrative approach may apply to the complexities of strategy implementation but sought to preserve more traditional rational underpinnings of strategic planning (Ireland & Hitt, 1997).

Adopting techniques of deconstruction like those championed by Derrida, Critical scholars have turned their attention to prominent artefacts in management education such as textbooks, which are depicted as 'instruments of [managerialist] propaganda' (Mir, 2003, p.734). Today, it is common for rebel teachers to contend that the textbook is a neocolonial instrument which suppresses alternative worldviews (Fougere & Moulettes, 2011). US textbooks are considered to be a prime source of propaganda, with the Critical view being that they present an ideal form of organisation which is capitalist in nature, and which reproduces Cold War narratives to dismiss more positive takes on communism and socialism (Foster et al., 2014).

In management education, the postmodern turn has prompted the introduction of deconstructive teaching techniques (Summers et al., 1997) as a means of enabling the marginal and repressed sides of a story which had previously been overlooked by the field (Boje, 2001). Today, deconstruction and other linguistic techniques serve as mainstays in investigating many of the issues around ethics and identity we will come across in the next two sections of this chapter on the Critical School.

While Critical scholars have sought to disrupt corporate production by entrenching an understanding of power structures and using linguistic methods for uncovering their techniques of oppression and marginalisation, the school also requires a rebel teacher for undertaking this work. Openly resistant to archetypes of authority, the shift to a Critical perspective in management education means a classroom educator who does away with many of the pedagogical techniques associated with Rational conceptions of the professor. No longer should the teacher be the central classroom figure, or sage on the stage, who has the knowledge and transmits it to groups of passive students (King, 1993). Instead, Freire prompts faculty to adopt a model where 'the teacher is no longer the-one-who-teaches, but who is himself [*sic*] taught in dialogue with the students' (Freire, 1972, p.53). This technique is now commonly referred as the guide on the side approach to teaching.

As has been discussed, this push for a new type of teacher appears to have gained momentum at the turn of the century through the moral failings of business school graduates leading companies engaged in scandal, such as Enron, Worldcom, and Arthur Andersen. At the time, senior Academy members became vocal in their argument that 'Faculty members need to own up to their own role in creating Enrons. It is their ideas that have done much to strengthen the practices they are all now so loudly condemning' (Ghoshal, 2003, p.21).

Equally, the 11 September 2001 terrorist attacks on the United States appear to have had a defining impact on the management education field and the role of the teacher. First, the attacks brought emotion and human strife to the classroom in a way never previously witnessed (Greenberg et al., 2002). Given that classes were in progress in vicinities near to the World Trade Center at the time of the attacks, educators felt a need to deal with their students' and their own feelings around what had occurred. Where classrooms in a traditional Rational pedagogical model were often kept as emotion-free zones, many professors chose to challenge this trend. Instead, they adopted a role which George Washington University faculty member Ruth Axelrod outlines as more like that of a counsellor (in Fukami, 2002). While the attacks occurred in New York, Washington DC, and the fields of Pennsylvania, they also perversely seemed to confirm a postmodern understanding of a world beyond that of the United States. A glance at published authors in the management education field demonstrates that it has now become open to a range of new voices and pedagogical techniques from outside the traditional US and western sphere, a process which appears to have accelerated since the Global Financial Crisis.

Where tinkerers in the Rational School consider how organisational skills can be taught, the focus of rebels in the Critical School has been to turn direction inward to the educator themself and acknowledgement of their own role in the process of capitalist production. Initially, this process meant taking a more activist role in changing the core values of business in specific topic areas such as environmental sustainability (Smith et al., 1994). However, Critical techniques have evolved and are now applied for helping educators understand their own role in the neoliberal production system, including the adoption of 'unsettling' practices designed to prompt critically reflexive identity work in examining underlying motives for action and the impact of those actions (Cunliffe, 2004; Knights et al., 2022). To this end, there has been little which has gone without critical review. From a spotlight on the marginalised role of the early career academic (Bristow et al., 2017), to the terror of publishing and performance targets (Jones et al., 2020), and to academic conferences as sites of extra-marital affairs, verbal violence (Spicer, 2005), and colonisation (Bell & King, 2010), the academic role has been deconstructed in numerous ways by Critical scholars.

Along with this interest in the inside world of the management educator has come a different understanding of the profession's calling. Where the Rational School would portray a morally detached educator, the Critical School pushes for a rebel teacher whose motivation is to emancipate others (Kogut et al., 2021). With a range of moral catastrophes laid by the Critical School at the feet of the neoliberal corporation, the result of this emancipatory intent is a more activist role. AMLE captures this shift through a recent editorial which encourages a move away from 'wilful ignorance' on the inequity promoted by economic growth, and towards a new model where management educators 'advocate for positive change' in cultivating 'a generative future for organizations, workers, and leaders' (Greenberg & Hibbert, 2022, p.166). This line of thinking on the role of the educator also implicates the need for teaching around topics of ethics.

UNDERSTANDING HOW OTHERS BEHAVE

The Critical School maintains a philosophical commitment to society, as evidenced in a growing set of pedagogies and practices around ethics in management education. The underlying ethical basis of Critical scholarship is a rights-based philosophy, with an explicit aim to provide a voice to the marginalised and repressed. Noteworthy in this movement are increasing commitments to social justice, and the implementation of feminist philosophies around an ethics of care. As rebel teachers have expanded their work in these areas, they have also increasingly raised questions around their own responsibilities as ethical guardians in business schools, and have sought to leverage their commitment to minority groups to raise questions about the business school and what they perceive as its underlying neoliberal foundations. By association, this critique of the business school has led to further assaults on the Rational School approach to management education.

The distinctive nature of the Critical School approach to ethics is its rejection of an overarching consequentialist ethical position, and its commitment to justice. Deriving from American philosopher John Rawls' *A Theory of Justice*, justice theories emphasise fairness as an overriding principle for facilitating the maximum benefit to marginalised and repressed members of society in instances where inequalities are present (Rawls, 1971).

While justice theories came to prominence through Rawls in the early 1970s, there is little early management education scholarship which provides a critical interpretation on matters involving ethics and sustainability. One exception is found in Lessam (1974), who advocates the work of some business schools in adopting a more emancipatory intent to their education by focusing on social responsibility and incorporating courses with titles such as 'Management and Mankind', and 'Management of Social Conflict'. Reflecting on the topic of social responsibility in education, Lessam calls for a Freire-style critical spirit through 'an awakening of individual awareness' (1974, p.18). He also sets out an implicit critique of the Rational School by providing steps for de-alienating students from what he perceives as misguided academic and scientific objectivity in management education. Pheysey (1980) continues in this spirit with a review of Salaman and Thompson's (1980) *Control and Ideology in Organizations* by criticising the authors' oversight in failing to present anti-organisation and radical organisation theory.

The same corporate crises in the 1980s such as Bhopal, which had driven the Rational School to respond with an increased focus on ethics, also appear to have prompted the emergence of a more critical take on ethics. Important to this push are contributions by Snell (1986, 1989) towards a critical agenda for ethics in management education and the principles on which it should be developed.

In the first piece, Snell (1986) sets out the need for management education to engage in greater dialogue on ethics. The author suggests such an agenda should require an understanding of ethical conduct which acknowledges a person's power to change their situations, a Critical commitment to questioning prevailing economic ideologies, and a deep concern for others. He argues for an ethical knowledge which incorporates an understanding of cultural and power differences in society.

In a follow-up piece, Snell (1989) advances a more explicitly socialist ethics for management education by referencing publications which might once have been considered too Marxist for the management education literature, such as the *New Socialist* (e.g. Jacobs, 1988) and *New Left Review* (e.g. Mobasser, 1987). According to Snell, socialist ethics should be built on principles of democracy, liberty, equality, and community. Consistent with rebel teacher interests in standing up for the marginalised and repressed, the model Snell advances rebuffs traditional shareholder models of profit maximisation by incorporating democratic principles to ensure that the organisation gives voice to the needs and interests of all employees and considers societal impacts when making resource decisions.

The then-radical nature of Snell's suggestion is for the organisation to make decisions which will prioritise groups beyond those they would normally give precedence. Snell advocates for decision making which focuses on the needs of stakeholders such as pensioners, children, and the unemployed. When it comes to liberty, Snell argues that the organisation must provide opportunity for workers to develop their own identity. In what appears to be a nod to future Critical management education trends around sexual identity, Snell opines, 'if someone can do the job well, should it matter if they don't behave like "real" men or women, and don't belong to certain social circles?' (1989, p.155). Snell continues that individuals should be allowed idiosyncrasies where their human growth and development are spurred by freedom from institutional order. Finally, management education ethics should be underpinned by a com-mitment to equality and community. This commitment entails a responsibility for the common good, including non-economic criteria for judging human progress, and organisational support of numerical minorities, such as those living with HIV.

Reflecting that 'the music of socialist values has, for the moment, been drowned under a deafening fanfare of opposing rhetoric and legislation' (1989, p.156), Snell perceives opportunity for the Critical School residing in the Gorbachev-era Soviet systems of *perestroika* and *glasnost* (Shannin, 1988). His view is that these approaches impel a push for justice, a better society, and more humane human beings. Importantly, Snell believes these emerging concepts might make it possible for organisations to move beyond dichotomies of capitalism and socialism, to create something new.

Pointers from the early 1990s suggest an emerging Critical approach to ethics in management education. While most management texts of the time remain indicative of Rational School scholarship, trends developed where foundational teaching materials began to incorporate chapters on business ethics and social responsibility. Social indicators from this period also support Snell's prediction of 'something new' between socialism and capitalism, with corporates such as accounting firm Arthur Andersen (perhaps ironically, given their later scandal-riven implosion) hosting summer ethics conferences for business faculty where they could be exposed to new ethical pedagogies and issues (Payne, 1993).

Meanwhile, notions of a postmodern world on which Critical scholars had sought to disrupt corporate production also gave rise to the idea of a 'postin-dustrial era' (Dauncey, 1988). Here, firms such as the Body Shop and Ben and Jerry's Ice Cream emerged as posterchildren for a shift towards environmental sustainability. Along with these new types of businesses came the suggestion that the dichotomy between planet and profit had been upended and that firms could be both green and profitable. From a management education perspective this development gave rise to a range of experiential techniques designed to develop a new generation of managers focused on sustainability. One example is found in the Frond Lake environmental role play developed by Moore and colleagues (1992). The role play revolves around a scenario in which students assume the role of manager at a pulp and paper mill. Facing a decision on whether to install anti-pollution equipment at a time when the firm is facing ongoing viability concerns, the scenario requires students to engage with complex choices around environmental sustainability and financial profitability (Moore et al., 1992). While the role play appears to be based on a more Rational pedagogy of building student skills, by concluding that the role play brings to the fore issues they may not have previously considered in the capitalist system, the authors provide a Critical bent to their work.

As previously discussed, the turn of the century presents a key moment in the development of the Critical School. The moral failure of business school graduates at the helm of scandal-hit firms such as Enron, Worldcom, and Arthur Andersen seems to have been important in affirming the Critical School's neoliberalist critique and its call for a greater emancipatory intent. Topics were now surfaced which would have been beyond the scope of Rational scholarship. Extending the notion of whistle-blower as raised in McCormick and Fleming's (1990) case on the potentially deficient missile technology, Kidwell and Kochanoswki (2005) sought to identify other types of workforce behaviour which might be considered both deviant but appropriate. The authors outline how behaviours such as withholding effort and employee theft might hold negative connotations for the organisation but may find justification through a wider moral benefit to society.

The nature of corporate failures at the turn of the Millennium also turned the heat on what were perceived as traditionally masculine forms of management and decision making. Hence, we see the emergence in management education of critical feminist theories, including what is known as an ethics of care. Distancing itself from the Rational School and its attempts to expand ethics in business education through stakeholder theory (Freeman, 1984), Critical theorists perceived the need for a more radical approach. Setting up the feminine firm as a moral enterprise to counter that of more traditional male-centred models (Dobson & White, 1995), proponents of a caring approach view it as a way of managing that focuses on relationships, consensus building, trust, and cooperation. At the heart of an ethics of care is the response to a stranger's problems of a feeling that 'I must do something', as an active obligation which is necessary for anyone who aspires to be moral (Burton & Dunn, 2005, p.459).

While ML had long held the Critical position that ethics could not be successfully taught without challenging the prevailing neoliberal paradigm (e.g.

Lessam, 1974), this perspective now also came to find a foothold in AMLE and JME. In what remains the most-cited piece in the history of AMLE, Ghoshal's (2005) final article prior to his passing takes aim at what he perceives as the denial of moral or ethical considerations in management theory. Ghoshal's polemic is followed by Giacalone and Thompson's (2006) push for a shift in management education away from an organisation-centred worldview based on increasing organisational wealth, to a human-centred worldview where physical and social well-being are prioritised.

Giacalone (2007) then takes the thinking inherent to this shift in perspective and applies it to an understanding of the rebel role of the management educator in preparing their students. His conclusion is that not only does the activist teaching role involve shaping the subject matter of their students, but that rebel teachers should also play a role in the types of students admitted to business studies, as well as those allowed to graduate. Referencing *The Matrix* (Wachowskis, 1999), a popular film in which the lead character takes a 'red pill' to discover truth about the illusions and deceptions of the world, Giacalone asserts the need for a similar antidote for business educators. Giacalone's 'red pill reality' is a world in which business educators supply 'organizations with the tools of their destruction – unethical students credentialed with our degrees who help to ruin organizations and the lives of countless stakeholders' (2007, p.534). He proposes a solution where educators opposed to the prevailing neoliberal worldview should wield their responsibility to certify the ethical worthiness of their students. Giacalone's argument is for management educators to become 'ethical sentinels', or gatekeepers, who impede the entry and graduation of students who might leverage their power and privilege to threaten the well-being of others.

From the activist rebel approach and feminist theories on an ethics of care emerges a focus on social justice. For Critical scholars, social justice is an emancipatory concept, where free individuals 'seek to extend related rights to ensure the social stability and harmony essential for everyone in current and future generations' (Caputo, 2002, p.356). A study by Toubiana (2012) finds that business school faculty possess a high degree of awareness and commitment to concerns of social justice around fairness and equity. However, the same study also shows that the institutional context created within the business school dilutes the personal meaning faculty has developed on these issues. The author finds that 'the extant hegemony identified within the participant's universities was preventing faculty from integrating their personal conceptualizations of social justice into the dominant logic of their Business Schools … [they were] prevented from expressing their personal convictions regarding businesses' purposes in their work and teaching' (Toubiana, 2012, p.96).

Recognising the barriers posed by the business school to the moral imperative of their work, Critical scholars turned their analytical attention to driving change in the business school itself. Where we have previously seen efforts at disrupting corporate production focused on features of management education such as the textbook (e.g. Mir, 2003; Foster et al., 2014), Critical scholars now focus on disintegrating dominant grand narratives of the business school (Parker, 2018a). Inspired by a range of critical studies on the university (e.g. Readings, 1996), Critical scholars consider the business school to be an intellectually fraudulent, greedy, profit-making engine of the university, and liken it to a lapdog of capital (Parker, 2018b). Perceptions emerge of neoliberal market forces which have created a business school sycophantic to multinational business and exploitative of academic careers (Jones et al., 2020). According to this view, academics are oppressed by an overarching bureaucracy which encourages bullying (Zawadzki & Jensen, 2020) and wreaks terror on its subjects through performance targets (McCann et al., 2020; Ratle et al., 2020).

For the Critical School, one remedy to the neoliberal business school is to undermine what they perceive as its overarching western ethnocentric and capitalist narratives. This approach means dismantling many of the assumptions on which the Rational School is based. As an example, Critical scholars have cast their eye over the Ford Foundation Report (Gordon & Howell, 1959) which had provided the skills-based underpinnings of the Rational School. Perceived as perpetuating a scientific research-based model of management education which values research rigour over relevance, Critical scholars have applied critical hermeneutic analysis to provide a counter-history of the report (McLaren, 2019). By arguing that elements of the report are inconsistent with a scientific model of knowledge and are anchored in early US responses to the Cold War, McLaren aims to dissipate the power held by Gordon and Howell and challenges audiences to move away from perpetuating its dominant narrative.

The Critical School has also taken aim at some key Rational School theories and pedagogies. These include Maslow's hierarchy, whose famous pyramid structure is claimed by Critical scholars to be a misinterpretation of Maslow's work and which was not initially illustrated in its pyramid incarnation by the man to whom it is credited. Critical scholars attribute the pyramid diagram to a consulting psychologist (McDermid, 1960) who had presented the heuristic as a way of making the theory easy to remember and then subsequently for making it scientifically testable (Bridgman et al., 2019).

Similarly, pedagogy as represented by the case study is shown by Critical scholars to have emerged from a history which is more contested than its proponents would have us believe (Bridgman et al., 2016). Where the technique has often been used as a mechanism for training future managers to solve narrow business problems of financial sustainability, deeper scrutiny by Critical scholars suggests its 1920s and 1930s development explicitly considered moral issues and included the voice of different stakeholders such as organised labour. Critical scholars argue that a return to the theoretical roots of case study development would support a more expansive case study pedagogy that considers social issues.

These efforts at uncovering marginalised and repressed histories have also culminated in different histories of business schools. Undermining what it perceives as a Rational School grand narrative of business schools as US-based institutions of science-based enquiry which came into their own through the Carnegie and Ford reports, the Critical School now offers far different inter-pretations. Histories of business schools have been developed which recognise the role of slavery in management education (Rosenthal, 2021), acknowledge history of Indigenous peoples (Doucette et al., 2021), outline the role of the Global South in developing different types of business schools (Zoogah, 2021; Wanderley et al., 2021), and consider how Black business schools have expanded management education to include roles in race and social welfare (Prieto et al., 2021). The call by Critical scholars in histories such as these is for business schools to move beyond prioritising economic goods and wealth accumulation and embrace change (McLaren et al., 2021).

Overall, the Critical School has maintained a commitment to improving the welfare of marginalised and repressed communities through its justice-based philosophy of ethics. It pursues this commitment through embedding ethics in classroom pedagogies, hearing the voices of those normally left out of management education, and undermining what it perceives as exploitative neoliberal practices of the Rational School. As the role of the rebel teacher has evolved, calls have come for educators to do more than just incorporate Critical perspectives into their classroom. As we have seen, some scholars now also argue for Critical scholars to act as ethical gatekeepers in ensuring students of a poor moral character are not allowed to graduate. The main way in which the Critical commitment to the marginalised and oppressed plays out is through becoming a champion of such groups. Hence, the next section on the push for equity in management education.

PUSHING FOR EQUITY

Critical scholarship in management education on the topic of identity enjoys a similar trajectory to that of ethics, where an initially slow uptake has turned into a rush of interest. This agenda has risen from a push away from US- and male-centred perspectives on management education, and a move towards equity. In this process, the Critical School has served to promote the legitimacy of minority groups, such as those with different sexual identities, as well as the perspectives of Indigenous people.

Given that the main source of diversity in western organisations in the 1970s and early 1980s arose from the influx of women in the workforce, early Critical scholarship on identity mainly reflects an interest with assisting this emerging segment. Yet where the Rational School focus on female workers portrayed a new element of the organisational workforce where integration would be required, the Critical School embraced this workplace movement as representing something quite different. The Critical approach is seen in Fonda's (1979) book review of *Making It in Management* (Fenn, 1978). Noting that women receive hostility in the workplace and are often prevented from managerial roles by social norms such as 'people won't work for a woman manager', Fonda argues that the Rational School approach of conflating the issue of women in the workforce within broader management issues is misplaced. Fonda therefore makes the case for a specialist understanding of women in the organisation.

Original works soon came to address the role of women in the organisation more critically. One piece by Davies frames the question, 'why are women not where the power is?' (1985, p.278). Identifying a power elite behind existing organisational structures, Davies presents the view that 'nothing short of a revolution' will affect the status quo (1985, p.278).

Another topic on which Critical scholars began to coalesce was the issue of race in the workforce. Like the move towards understanding women as a unique workplace group, this scholarship seeks to move beyond notions of integration by characterising racial groups as unique and requiring their own ways of being managed. Black voices began to be heard, offering their own experiences in organisational settings. Along these lines, Jones (1994) presents her own encounters with usurping taken-for-granted stereotypes around who should be a management education teacher. In the opening lines of her piece on diversity appreciation she begins, 'I cannot mask my essence. One of the first things that other people notice is that I am an African American woman. What is not obvious is that I am a college professor' (Jones, 1994, p.432).

This move towards hearing and understanding minority voices receives further prominence in the post-Millennium period, where Critical School scholarship assumes a more visible position in the management education literature. As we have seen, where the Rational School had developed pedagogies in the 1990s designed around equality and intended to assist often white, male managers in managing minority segments of the workforce, the rise of the Critical School evidences a different approach. A defining issue is the push by Critical scholars against the notion of equality, a construct they believe is insufficient for overcoming sexual and racial oppressions of the organisation. Instead, rebel teachers push for an equity approach on matters of identity.

Similar to the ethics of care which had emerged at the start of the Millennium as a feminist response to what proponents perceived as the masculine ethical culture of the period, Critical scholars also seek to make visible what they perceive as the masculine power structures inherent to the study of organisations.

Feeling restricted by 'palatable arguments' around equal employment opportunity or diversity, Sinclair (2000) puts forward an approach for considering gender relations in organisations by focusing on masculinities.

Drawing on an emerging wider interest in organisation theory on masculinity and privilege (e.g. Kerfoot & Knights, 1993), Sinclair focuses on masculinity as an invisible organisational phenomenon which gains powerful ascendency to deny other perspectives around topics such as women in leadership. Sinclair sets out the case that masculine power structures either deny that the absence of women from senior levels is a serious issue, or explain this absence as a result of women failing to adapt to male norms. To overcome masculine power structures, the author sets out a classroom approach where she highlights to male students how they are imprisoned by traditional male stereotypes around issues such as being pressured back to work after a baby, or not being able to talk about the death of a child. In her efforts to address masculinities, Sinclair also sets out a course structure which supports reflection, creates an open environment for students to voice doubts and expose vulnerabilities, and involves men as examples and allies.

In the following year, Lorbiecki (2001) charts changing views on the concept of diversity. Noting the rise to prominence of diversity frameworks in institutions such as the European Union, Lorbiecki expresses critical doubt that the prevailing diversity movement can improve workplace equality. Suggesting that workplace equality programmes do little more than encourage women and people of colour to 'fit in', the author argues for a learning perspective on diversity in which minorities are encouraged to bring to the workplace their different backgrounds and perspectives on how to do work. Lorbiecki's thesis is that these alternative positions will challenge normative assumptions and emancipate organisations from the views of white, middle-class males.

This changing paradigm encourages rebel teachers to turn a reflexive lens on their own role in perpetuating existing power structures. In an early example of a theme which was to be explored many times over the next decade and a half, Macalpine and Marsh (2005) turn the lens on themselves as white management educators to highlight business schools as creating a body of knowledge which they believe lacks understanding on race. Reaffirming an emerging consensus that equality and diversity initiatives are inadequate for changing organisational practices about race, Macalpine and Marsh advocate for organisations to engage in a process of active 'colouring' which will treat race as a verb, rather than a noun. This approach is aimed at disrupting the white right to supremacy the authors perceive as implicit in organisational beliefs and mental models promoted by the management education field.

This more activist Critical approach to upending taken-for-granted paradigms in organisations and management education is reflected in several areas. From Simpson's (2006) efforts at feminising the MBA, to exploring gaps between practical and discursive consciousness on issues of gender in organisations (Mathieu, 2009), Critical attempts to upend the status quo by introducing previously marginalised or suppressed voices have become widely published management education practice.

These efforts were soon also targeted at the US-centred nature of management education. Neal and Finlay (2008) take aim at what they see as hegemony over the developing world of American values and ideologies in management education. Notable is that this piece is published in JME, previously a bastion of the Rational School. Here we see new audiences introduced to Critical terms such as hegemony and power. The Critical attack on US values and frameworks has also heralded a shift to a post-colonial classroom where multiple voices are heard. This approach is captured by Harney and Linstead (2009), who work to overcome vestiges of white European Christianity in management education by introducing Latin American, African, and Asian ideas of liberation theology. Liberation theology represents a movement which sets itself against Christianity by portraying Jesus as human rather than God, and by depicting early Christian communities as communist.

While issues of ethnicity and gender have remained prominent, most notable for the Critical School in the post-2010 period has been the steps taken in advancing scholarship around issues of sexual identity. Where gender and sexuality had been treated as immutable by the Rational School, the Critical School has introduced new understanding of sexual identity as shifting and fluid. This Critical approach is taken up by McDonald (2013), who uses the concept of queer reflexivity to detail his coming out as a gay male while doing ethnographic research on a sexual health organisation. Discussing his engagement with queer theory in helping to make sense of this organisation and his own relationship to it, McDonald outlines his shift from normative discourses on being straight, to an emerging realisation that he is gay and he therefore details his coming out announcement to friends and family.

In subsequent years, new types of sexual identity have come to the Critical management education agenda. Rudin and colleagues (2016) introduce a pedagogical innovation to reduce transphobia, a discrimination based on gender identity rather than sexual orientation. Acting in advance of US employment discrimination laws where the trans community had not been offered the same protections as gay, lesbian, and bisexual communities, the authors provide a case study involving conflict between two co-workers over the choice of an organisational restroom. One of the workers in the scenario is a transgender person. Noting that access to bathrooms of their choice is an important issue for transgender people, the authors set the students to play the role of CEO in an organisation receiving a complaint from a female worker about sharing the same restroom as a co-worker transitioning from a male to female sexual identity.

Building on these understandings of sexual identities as shifting and non-binary, Rumens (2017) attempts to destabilise LGBTIQA+ identities by examining them through the lens of queer theory. Lamenting the homosexual/heterosexual binary which had featured in management education, Rumens aims to incorporate a performative and permanently open queer understanding of identity. Drawing on Butler (e.g. 2004), Rumens argues that gender is performed within pre-existing sets of discourses, or norms, that are always in the process of being remade. Stepping beyond that which would have been imaginable to members of the Rational School, this performative understanding leads to a critical question around identity: What are the conditions of the possibility of your becoming (Cabantous et al., 2015)? This line of thinking encourages Rumens to ask key questions of management educators, such as the limits posed by pedagogical discourses on how LGBTIQA+ identities are understood, the effects of heteronormative and cisnormative assumptions on current pedagogical practices, and how management educators can act as allies for LGBTIQA+ students.

While Critical School studies in race, sex, and sexual identity have done much to destabilise the white, male, middle-class underpinnings of management education, it is not until more recently that Indigenous perspectives have emerged from beyond the periphery of identity studies. This situation has changed from the late 2010s, where a range of scholarship now attempts to decolonise knowledge by bringing Indigenous voices on learning and place to bear on new understandings around management and learning. Critical scholars have subsequently introduced a range of non-western perspectives to the management education field, including New Zealand Māori ways of thinking, feeling, and behaving (Tangihaere & Twiname, 2011), and the use of encounters with Hindu CEOs in India to drive dislocation and surprise in thinking about management education theory and teaching (Schwabenland, 2011).

Other examples include the introduction by Pio and Syed (2020) of the Ashokan (ancient Indian) legacy of dhamma, or effective connection, for better reframing understanding on the topic of diversity. Picking up on the centrality of language and discourse as the basis of knowledge in the Critical School and emerging themes on indigeneity, Doucette and colleagues (2021) also bring to the literature American and Canadian Indigenous perspectives for developing a conversational approach which injects Indigenous people and their perspectives to management education.

Where Indigenous perspectives might once have been perceived as more naturally attuned to addressing issues of environmental sustainability (e.g. Banerjee, 2011), these new discourses have also been used to destabilise western ethnocentric interpretations of the business school. Woods and colleagues (2022) outline their efforts at indigenising the entrepreneurial education curricula so that it is inclusive of Indigenous voices and perspectives. Through an understanding of decolonisation as a process which makes explicit colonial domination and hierarchies of power, the authors outline their experience in engaging with Māori pedagogy, known as *ako*. Explaining how this approach adopts a reciprocal learning between teacher and student, the authors outline how the role of teacher comes to be about 'creating contexts for learning where the students can enter the learning conversation' (Woods et al., 2022, p.87). This pedagogical context introduces the Māori value system of *whakapapa*, which promotes belonging through relationships and collective notions of success. While the authors' entrepreneurship course retains mainstream western frameworks such as the Business Model Canvas (Blank, 2013), the interspersion of Māori business case studies and cultural frameworks for innovation through the course content provides the authors with the ability to engage with and regenerate Indigenous ways of knowing.

In May 2020, the issue of race and white privilege in management education was brought to the fore by the murder of the Black man George Floyd by a white, male police office in Minneapolis. Reflective of an apparent metamorphosis towards being a more Critical journal, JME presents a special issue on privilege in management education. This collection advances the view that management educators often enjoy an unearned and sustained advantage based on their race, gender, sexual orientation, socioeconomic status, or age (Leigh & Rivers, 2023).

To overturn dominant white narratives in management education, the special issue brings a range of marginalised and repressed voices to attention. These articles include Ferraro's (2023) use of counter-storytelling to disrupt what the author contends is the privileging of whites and men by the management education field. Presenting a typical classroom interaction in her Introduction to Critical Race Theory (CRT) class, Ferraro illustrates an approach for critiquing economic systems of power when teaching about Black women's activism and enterprise.

Ferraro's approach is to ask students to debate the concept of meritocracy. The first student responds that meritocracy is a myth that people get what they deserve, while the second argues it is about children being born into the right family. Reflecting on these responses, Ferraro (2023, p.40) suggests 'I was happy that the framework elicited this kind of discussion, but I knew we had to go further'. As next steps, she investigates perceived biases in mechanisms such as SAT (university entry) scores and presents a critique of neoliberal capitalism as inherently exploitative and responsible for embedding persistent inequity (Marable, 2015).

Another article in the same special issue brings attention to the pedagogy around teaching CRT. Lo (2023) addresses the issue of intersectionality, or the experience of being both privileged and marginalised inherent in his identities as a gay man of Asian descent, embedded in a more entitled academic culture.

Reflecting on his experience in teaching courses in international business, organisational behaviour, and race, Lo details a pedagogical process where he leverages books such as *White Rage* (Anderson, 2016) and *Me and White Supremacy* (Saad, 2020) to upend dominant white male narratives. Introducing an experiential understanding of privilege, Lo details a classroom practice of unlearning 'everything we know about race', anchored in reflective practice on eight questions based around histories and ideologies of a student's lived experience in self-identified marginalised groups. Introducing examples of identity characteristics which lack privilege in the United States, Lo extends understanding of intersectionality beyond race, gender, and sexual orientation to include body size, height, mental wellness, and neurodiversity.

In this push for equity, we can therefore see how rebel teachers have responded over time to champion those without a voice. From an interest which once focused on women and racial minorities in the workplace, the Critical School now pursues topics in sexual identity and indigeneity. These new areas of identity have brought into management education a range of new theories and perspectives, such as the fluidity of sexual identity viewed through the lens of queer theory, as well as Indigenous notions around entrepreneurship and sustainability. As the Critical School continues to work towards breaking down western traditions and taken-for-granted assumptions, Lo's (2023) work is important in identifying some of the next likely horizons, including dismantling barriers imposed on people of differing body shapes, and people with neurodivergent diagnoses such as ADHD and autism. Overall, it is likely that the interests of the management education field on the topic of identity have some way to run.

CONCLUSION

In reflecting on the evolution of the Critical School from a niche area to perhaps the dominant school in management education, it is possible to observe two key features. First, much Critical scholarship provides an outright repudiation of the Rational School. Where Rational scholarship takes a largely uncritical eye to the corporation, Critical scholarship establishes the neoliberal firm as a vehicle of environmental, sexual, and racial exploitation. Therefore, where tinkerer teachers aim to prepare students for the workplace, rebel teachers aim to emancipate them from oppressive underlying power structures of western institutions such as the corporation. Hence, we see teaching which aims to make visible the often-invisible structural power dynamics inherent to traditional institutions, including business schools and management education, and provides students with the pedagogical means for emancipation.

The second key feature of the Critical School is around the role of the teacher. Teachers in this school have a moral imperative to act in the interests of society, and to set up pedagogical techniques which draw out the repressed voices that would otherwise be marginalised or overlooked. In this pursuit, there can be no such thing as the morally detached teacher. Instead, the rebel teacher must assume an activist position, and should engage in critical reflexivity to identify their own underlying privileges and power. The Critical scholar is therefore always about breaking down tradition.

This position is relevant to our next school, the Postliberal School, which contrasts itself with the Critical School by setting itself out as being a defender of tradition.

QUESTIONS FOR THE READER

1. Quickly write down your three immediate takes on the foundations of the Critical School. Do these foundations match your own beliefs and values on management education?
2. To what extent do you feel like a rebel teacher, seeking to upset the status quo? How is this outlook evidenced in your teaching?
3. Early Critical scholarship in management education on the topic of power maintained the possibility of a positive view of authority. Do you agree with this possibility? Or do you see authority as something from which to flee?
4. In your own reading of management education, have you noticed a shift to a more activist approach to teaching? Which article have you read that best captures this shift?
5. Giacalone (2007) proposes that educators should adopt the role of 'ethical sentinels', with a responsibility to impede the entry and graduation of students who might leverage their power and privilege to threaten the well-being of others. How do you feel about the ethical sentinel role? Is it one you would adopt, or have adopted, in your own career?
6. Bridgman, Cummings & Ballard (2019) have shown that the history of Maslow's hierarchy is different to what we have been informed by management education textbooks. Is there a theory or framework you teach which you have taken for granted? Return to the original literature piece on this theory and re-evaluate it. Identify three key messages you might now convey in your teaching because of the greater breadth of understanding you have developed on the subject.
7. Thinking of your own teaching, are there any minority perspectives you have included in your own classroom? What has provided the basis for this perspective? Was it founded in your own personal identity?
8. Using the checklist of identity features provided by Lo (2023), document your own intersectionality. Reflect on what your own intersectional characteristics mean for your teaching.

5. A brief (and incomplete) history of the Postliberal School

The foolish educator strode into the art museum where he had scheduled his class for the opening week. Maybe this time would be different? Maybe there would be a group of students who weren't there just to attain some credentials and exit into the workforce as quickly as possible? Maybe there might be more than just the students who were there to do good for society? Whatever that even meant. He rolled his eyeballs as he entered. If anyone noticed, he didn't care. Today's topic on virtues and vices was so far away from what they would be expecting that he knew he would receive complaints. What was he going to do? Stand up and tell them all about how to manage something like climate change using data analytics? Tell them about how they needed to tear down every last vestige of anything they had ever held dear like their family and their community and start again? Or actually delve into who they were as human beings, including their strengths and weaknesses and realise that they all had much more in common than the media and pretty much everyone else was telling them? He listened as the art curator introduced the exhibit before which the class found themselves. There was the painting captured in black and white tones featuring a pair of eyes peering out from behind a curtain, a single tear tracing down the subject's cheek. The foolish educator piped up, 'what do you take from this piece of work?' A young woman in the front row leaned forward in her seat, 'that's like me after a bad assignment score, it just doesn't show the bottle of wine I drank afterwards'. Laughter broke out around the room. The foolish educator congratulated himself. The group was starting to connect as human beings.

INTRODUCTION

While the Postliberal label has not been previously applied to the field, there is a small undercurrent of management education scholarship which appears to reflect a wider philosophical movement attacking progressive liberalism from traditional perspectives (e.g. Deneen, 2018; Milbank & Pabst, 2016). The Postliberal School of management education has rarely represented more than a niche area in the management education literature.

Postliberals present a critique of liberalism. For Postliberals such as Adrian Pabst, liberalism is a broad concept, but can most readily be conceived as an approach to society which emphasises the primacy of the individual (Spencer, 2021). Pabst argues that liberal market democracy presents an illusion of markets as generating prosperity for everyone, 'while in reality enforcing monopoly and enriching a new oligarchic class of "professionals" led by financiers' (2019, p.35). Blond provides a more acerbic take of a 'perverted and endlessly corrupting liberalism' (2010, p.139). In that economic liberalism features in authoritarian and populist regimes in India, Russia, and China, Pabst reflects on it as 'really politically quite promiscuous, I mean it's happy to get into bed with pretty much anyone' (Spencer, 2021).

To the Postliberal, the Critical and Rational schools present different sides of the same coin in that they both perpetuate a liberal, rampantly individualistic society which works to destroy any shared approach to life. The way in which liberalism advances is through myths of rational and inevitable progress, and a rejection of the history of all which has come before it. Postliberals therefore attempt at reviving traditional communitarian understandings of the world. Where the Critical scholar seeks to disintegrate all forms of tradition, the emphasis from Postliberals is on institutions where humans can gain shared meaning – the family, the community, the church, and the nation.

In the 1970s and 1980s, contrarian educational scholars such as Denis Pym, Jerry Harvey, and Peter Vaill all set out a distinctly anti-progressive approach to educating students, which perhaps found its high-water mark in Vaill's *Learning as a Way of Being: Strategies for Survival in a World of Permanent White Water* (1996). Today, the Postliberal School appears largely crowded out of the management education field by Critical School scholarship. But as concerns mount over the negative effects of corporations and technology on natural environments and human populations, the Postliberal School offers a potential haven for scholars who conclude that something must be done, but who maintain philosophical objections to the disintegrative approach of the Critical School.

The Postliberal image of the educator is one of fool or rogue. This picaro-style character lives at the margins of contemporary society, which it believes has corrupted or lost essential values. The modus operandi of the picaro character is therefore to use absurd actions and humour for making society an object of satire (Ballinger, 1991–1992). Despite facing a range of challenges, picaro characters do undertake an arc of character development, a feature brought home to contemporary management education by James March in applying the character of Don Quixote to help students understand the nature of leadership (Augier, 2004).

A more contemporary fool comes in the form of Ignatius J. Reilly, a character from John Kennedy Toole's Pulitzer Prize-winning *A Confederacy of Dunces* (1980). Anti-hero Reilly is a troublemaker and dreamer non-conformist. Similar to the Postliberal educator seeking to revive classical or religious traditions such as virtue (MacIntyre, 1981), Reilly inhabits two worlds: the contemporary one which he despises and seeks to educate, and a classical medieval world which he seeks to revive. Reilly's absurdist rampage through New Orleans, which involves a botched attempt at fermenting factory worker insurrection, selling hot dogs while dressed as a pirate, and accidentally uncovering a racket for distributing pornographic photos to the city's high schools (Kline, 1999), is reminiscent of the Postliberal educator's attempts at being a teacher while learning to not teach (Harvey, 1979). To the extent Reilly represents more than parody, it is in his embodiment of the 'conflict between pragmatic reality as the contemporary world sees it and a more mystic one as the medievalists saw it' (Bell, 1988, p.17), a feature again prominent in Postliberal management educator Jerry Harvey and his ongoing scriptural meditations in the workplace (Harvey, 1988).

The Postliberal view is therefore of an education system drawn into this culture of liberalist exploitation. Elite universities draw students into careerist education where they are inculcated to embrace identity politics, diversity, potentiality, and permanent placelessness for furthering their own economic interests (Deneen, 2018). In contrast, the Postliberal values an education which embraces the notion of limits by emphasising student formation, essence, and nature (Carlin, 2021a). The idea of limits places the Postliberal School squarely at odds with the Rational and Critical schools, which both maintain an ideal based in the unbounded potential of the individual. The following section explores in greater detail the underlying foundations of the Postliberal School world.

POSTLIBERAL SCHOOL FOUNDATIONS

The world of the Postliberal School is based on a divine metaphysics, an affinity with the traditional, virtue ethics, and an understanding of authority as the freedom to. These foundations are set out in Figure 5.1.

The basis of knowledge for the Postliberal rests in a divine metaphysics. To the Postliberal there is a God, there is a natural order, and there are things which are simply unknowable. Hence, the importance to this school of cultural and religious tradition (Carlin, 2021a). This view of the world explains some of the names we can see in the line of Postliberal thought including, Aristotle, C.S. Lewis, Thomas Aquinas, Augusto Del Noce, Simone Weil, Antonio Rosmini, Alasdair MacIntyre, Michael Sandel, and Wendell Berry. Postliberals believe there are ultimate questions around topics such as death or guilt, to which only God can give an answer. For the Postliberal there are metaphysical absolutes, a logos, or divine order of being that lies within all creation (Carlin, 2021b). For this reason, they believe there is a need for 'God and the Church and the pastor' (Del Noce & Lancellotti, 2017, p.51).

This understanding of the world has important effects on the empirical foundation of Postliberal scholarship. Postliberals are critical of the Enlightenment project for producing a Rational liberalism based on natural science as the only true form of knowledge. While Postliberals do not quarrel with science

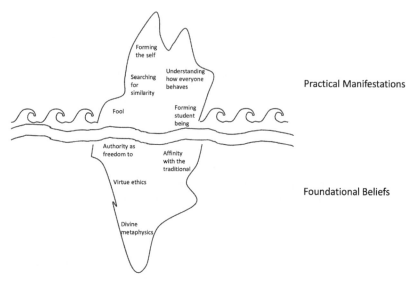

Figure 5.1   *The world of the Postliberal School*

as applied in the biological and physical sciences, they remain concerned at how science has been elevated to the study of economic and social phenomena (such as management education), where it provides answers to questions which Postliberals believe are simply unknowable. While Postliberals maintain enthusiasm for the natural sciences (Del Noce & Lancellotti, 2015), they believe there is a human nature, or an essence, which can never be fully understood by human minds through psychological and sociological research (Carlin, 2021a). For the Postliberal, social science is scientistic, defined as:

> mechanical and uncritical application of habits of thoughts to those different from those in which they have been formed. The scientistic as distinguished from the scientific view is not an unprejudiced but a very prejudiced approach which, before it has considered its subject, claims to know what is the most appropriate way of investigating it. (Hayek, 1942, p.269)

The product of this scientistic approach is a technological society, in which the capitalism of the Rational School and the Marxism of the Critical School have combined. As Deneen explains, an 'unholy marriage between Marx and Ayn Rand' (2022), where scientism, technology, and markets merge to create a world in which all relations are material, and where this full exploitation of natural resources serves to 'eliminate completely the distinction between free men and slaves' (Del Noce & Lancellotti, 2015, p.12). This view pits the Postliberal against both the Rational and Critical schools, which they believe engage in efforts to deny nature. In a dry take on the distinction between man and nature, Lewis (1975) details a recent conversation in which one person declared 'man has nature whacked'. Lewis continues, 'in their context the words had a certain tragic beauty, for the speaker was dying of tuberculosis' (1975, p.67).

Perceiving an endlessly exploitative capitalist society in which all human relations are material (Del Noce & Lancellotti, 2015), Postliberals view a return to tradition as the only solution to societal ills. The dichotomy between liberalism and tradition is captured by philosopher Wendell Berry in his depiction between what he calls exploiters and nurturers. Tracing a history in the United States involving perceived subjugation of American Indians, small farms and communities, local tradesmen, independent craftsmen, and, finally, households of citizens, Berry argues that this exploitation stems from commercial trade which first involved furs and now involves technology, weapons, and drugs (Berry, 2015). For Berry, the exploiter is a person such as a strip miner, someone motivated by profit who wishes to earn as much as possible by as little work as possible and who values a piece of land only by its potential to produce. In contrast, the nurturer values their own, their family's, their community's, and their country's health, and they expect to earn a decent living from their work, which involves activity which won't diminish their land (Berry, 2018).

While the Postliberal School is the least prominent of the schools in management education, its image of the educator as a fool who holds a mirror up to society offers a different approach on the role of the educator to that of the Rational and Critical schools. Postliberals shy away from the tag of teacher, and instead consider themselves as learners (Harvey, 1979). Their reluctance to consider themselves as teachers is related to their metaphysical understanding of the world, and their position that the original teacher is Jesus Christ.

As an example, when Mary Magdalene recognises the risen Jesus at the burial tomb, 'she turned and said to him in Hebrew, "Rabbouni"! (which means teacher)' (New Revised Standard Version, 2023, John 20, verse 16). Of note is that Jesus Christ is the only one in the Gospel of Matthew whose actions are labelled as teaching. Those handpicked by Jesus to follow him are called disciples. The word disciples is a translation of the Greek *mathetes*, which literally means 'learner' (Perrin, 1974). It is only in the final two verses of the Gospel of Matthew where Jesus has been resurrected and is near to heavenly ascension that the disciples are encouraged to teach. Jesus says to the disciples, 'Go therefore and make disciples of all nations, baptising them in the name of the Father and of the Son and of the Holy Spirit, and teaching them to obey everything that I have commanded you' (New Revised Standard Version, 2023, Matthew 28, verses 19–20).

If the central defining question for management educators is how they relate to the corporation, then the Postliberal School takes a different position to those of the Rational and Critical schools. Postliberals are similar to Critical scholars in their perception of organisations as corrosive institutions on society. They present a cynical view of organisations, which they compare to swamps and frog farms (Harvey, 1977), and where some organisational actors are even likened to Nazis (Harvey, 1988). However, Postliberals are also critical of the other schools for their emphasis on the primacy of the individual (Spencer, 2021). This approach means that while the Critical School aims to address neoliberalism by disintegrating traditional institutions, the Postliberal position is to revive institutions devoted to a shared common humanity such as the family, community, church, and nation.

The underlying ethics of the Postliberal School is a philosophical transcendental theology, resulting in virtue ethics. The combination of this philosophy and ethics means that Postliberal education is less interested in teaching trends and topics, and more aligned with an emphasis on the formation of student being. The Postliberal educator therefore works at putting in place systems for drawing out student character and virtue. In adopting this position, Postliberals reject relativist and consequentialist ethics as inherently unethical. This argument is set out in Carlin (2021b), who leverages Del Noce to trace a lineage of these two ethical systems as forms of modern Gnosticism.

The task of a foolish educator is therefore to set up learning experiences for assisting students to understand themselves. Here, notions of virtue and character are fundamental. For Postliberals such as Peter Vaill (1996), a world of permanent change means that the most effective form of learning is for students to understand their own presence in the world. This approach is based on an understanding that, as humans, we are all characterised by a range of vices and virtues. Our way of knowing and being in the world is therefore best supported by understanding our own strengths and weaknesses and working within these constraints.

Postliberals therefore present a starkly different educational intent to the other two schools. The Rational and Critical schools have embraced an education of becoming, where 'the ascent to God is replaced by the idea that one can conquer the world, that each individual is entitled to do so' (Del Noce & Lancellotti, 2015, p.46). In contrast, the Postliberal School adopts the primacy of being. Here, Postliberals see limits to education and the benefit of subordinating one's own instinctual individual desires to that of traditional communitarian sources of growth and freedom as found in the family, church, and nation (Carlin, 2021a). The educational task is therefore to facilitate student formation, where the individual becomes anchored in a reality of self and circumstances and is inspired to develop their inner self, unity with others, and service to others, in expressing their full potential (Lips-Wiersma & Morris,

2017). Handy identifies those coming from this philosophical tradition as more interested in pupils than subjects and notes their purpose in drawing out talents out of individuals while remaining true to their own values (1975).

To the extent that the Postliberal School is apparent in management education, it is visible through pedagogies which explore virtue and character (Hartman, 2006), or which utilise techniques such as poetry and irony to draw out people's understanding of themselves (Van Buskirk & London, 2012). Postliberals also use classical techniques more consistent with a traditional humanities education. It is noteworthy that Sparks' (2017) piece on the classroom of Postliberal management educator Jerry Harvey includes a depiction of students writing poems, performing songs, and playing musical instruments.

Where the Critical School presents a wholly negative take on authority, the Postliberal School perceives the concept in a positive light. For Italian philosopher Augusto Del Noce, authority is the concept which has most been corrupted by the secularisation of the liberal society. Del Noce argues that Critical ambitions for emancipation have stripped the notion of authority of its intended and original conceptual distinction. Tracing the etymological concept to its linguistic origins in his native Italian, Del Noce links authority to words such as 'Augustus (he who makes grow), auxilium (help provided by a higher power), augurium (also a word of religious origin: a vow to obtain divine cooperation in growth' (Del Noce and Lancellotti, 2015, p.189). Casting a wider net, Del Noce also notes that German and Gothic languages emphasise this notion of authority as to make grow.

The distinction between these understandings of growth and modern secular interpretations of authority are important. Where authority in the more traditional sense is a positive concept which recognises in the family the ability of the mother and the father to hand down values and help, in the contemporary sense authority represents only a state of subjection which represses human growth and must therefore be escaped. Given that Del Noce saw the path to this secular society most clearly in the French student revolutions of 1968 from which the Critical School gained its inspiration, he associates with the hippie movement a perspective on freedom as freedom from the burden of all moral obligations associated with traditional family, community, and national notions of authority.

The nature of authority for the Postliberal educator is illustrated by Vaill (1997). Reflecting on his ambition to reduce the power distance between himself and his students, he aims to provide his students with freedom. Importantly, this is different to the emancipatory freedom which characterises the Critical School. Instead, it represents freedom through authority in the interests of developing a shared humanity.

> [Freedom] is not a laissez-faire, do-whatever-you-please atmosphere. Rather, I want participants to need to spend as little energy as possible figuring out how to 'play the game' of one of my sessions. For me, the 'game' is that there is no game apart from our mutual engagement with each other through the subject matter. My hope is that this will free participants to focus on the subject matter that brings us together. (Vaill, 1997, p.273)

The Postliberal School is a fledgling one in management education. Indeed, it appears to be nearly extinct. The school has always represented a niche area in management education, but is represented by publications from scholars such as Gib Akin, Peter Vaill, and Jerry Harvey in early pieces from the *Journal of Management Education* (JME) (e.g. Harvey, 1979; Vaill, 1981). However, the approach seems to have reached its peak in the mid-1990s with the publication of Peter Vaill's (1996) *Learning as a Way of Being.* Since then, there appears to have been a decline in publication of works with a discernibly Postliberal flavour. Possible causes include the rising popularity of the Critical School in the post-Millennium period, as well as the rejection of empirical methods in social science by foolish educators. The latter move away from empirical methods causes challenges for Postliberals in publishing via traditional journal outlets. It is noteworthy that both Jerry Harvey and Peter Vaill were more published in books than journal articles (Dent, 2022; Middleton & Alday, 2023).

This chapter will introduce the Postliberal School. We will see how it rejects engagement with the organisation by focusing on a learning of being over becoming (Carlin, 2021a), and by fashioning a role for the teacher more akin to that of a character in the medieval court. The chapter will also outline the ethical basis of the Postliberal School through advocacy of a return to Greek and Roman traditions of Aristotelan virtue, and the rejection of the rights approach found in the Critical School. Finally, we will see how this approach plays out in topics of identity, where foolish educators seek to anchor learning around a search for a deeper shared humanity involving reflection, sympathy, and pedagogies for encouraging personal formation.

FORMING THE SELF

The Postliberal approach to education is to set parameters under which the student can form their own self. Rejecting the Rational School typology of the tinkerer preparing students for the workplace, and the Critical School typology of the rebel trying to disintegrate the western ethnocentric corporation, the Postliberal instead focuses on the student themselves.

Anchored in thought dating back to Plato and his philosophies around becoming (that which is engaged in continuous change) versus being (that which does not undergo becoming) (Bolton, 1975), the Postliberal rejects education based on a philosophy of becoming. Vaill sets out this approach by arguing that the only way for students to survive a world of constant change and surprise is for them to engage with learning as a way of being. Instead of uniform teaching of workplace skills, learning as a way of being is 'idiosyncratic and subjective to each individual' (Vaill, 1996, p.51). The foolish educator therefore aims to help students understand themselves through pedagogies such as self-directed and creative learning which focus on the essence of the learner.

Postliberal educators embrace the notion of limits, where there is no promise of endless improvement and there is virtue in recognising our own (and nature's) inherent boundaries on what is possible (Carlin, 2021a). A starting point for the foolish educator is often to recognise their own limits. Athos (1979) details such thinking: 'I thought with time my weaknesses would decrease and my strengths would increase. That's not true. It has been a bipolar development. The things I'm good at get better and the things I'm worse at get even worse as time goes on' (Athos, 1979, p.7).

Foolish educators focus on the essence of the learner. The primacy of being for the Postliberal educator is summarised by Vaill in his call for the Organisation Behaviour lecturer to 'embody and exude a sense of the species' fascination and delight with itself' (1979, p.4). The approach extends beyond that typically found in the classroom to encompass all aspects of a person's life, including their self-awareness and the state of their unconscious minds. An illustration of how the foolish educator pursues such an endeavour can be found in the description by Athos (1979) on the energy he expends on knowing and understanding students' socioeconomic backgrounds, their concerns, their interests, and even impacts on their mood of the weather.

In distinguishing between learning approaches based on having and being, Maclagan (1991) offers insights into the Postliberal approach to education. Where the having approach is about exercising mastery over other living things and increasing what one possesses, the being approach is about giving up egocentricity and the desire for things through the need for being at one with others. In a JME piece, Ramsey and Fitzgibbons (2005) set out a classroom practice based on being rather than doing. Declaring their philosophical affinity to the spiritually infused educational approach of Parker Palmer, the authors discuss their efforts to develop being with students. Their pedagogy rests on the central understanding that 'students control their own learning' (Ramsey & Fitzgibbons, 2005, p.338) and captures a story-based learning experience based on students' personal accounts of their experiences in work and organisations.

The task for the Postliberal educator is therefore to provide students with conditions which will encourage the emergence and development of their natural essence. For foolish educators this means there is emphasis on phronesis over episteme. Traced back to Aristotle, the notion of phronesis means a move away from knowledge which is universal and generally applicable, back to practical wisdom which is virtuous and contextual (Flyvbjerg, 2001). Phronesis is something which emerges through situated everyday action and is a continuous and non-heroic form of practice (Hahn & Vignon, 2019).

One approach which allows students to form their own character can be found in self-directed learning, where the student is put at the centre of the learning process. Consistent with the Postliberal emphasis on the nature of the individual, self-directed learning moves the educational process away from course content and towards the process of learning. Human essence is captured in the pedagogy of self-directed learning by the underlying pedagogical assumption that human beings grow in their capacity to be self-directing as they mature (Akin, 1991). In setting up a self-directed learning experience, management educators aim to provide students with the opportunity to reflect (Rhee, 2003), and to determine their own strengths and weaknesses (Boyatzis, 1994).

Creative learning is another pedagogy used by Postliberal scholars to focus on the essence of the individual. In a creative learning approach, it is not possible to know where the learning is going and when it has 'gotten there' (Vaill, 1996, p.62). Vaill notes that an important component of the creative learning approach is the idea of surprise, because it is when the learner hits surprising moments that the learning occurs. Hence, Van Buskirk and London (2008) argue that the poetry and poetic metaphors they leverage in their teaching create a more personal and intense context for learning because of the capacity for surprise that poetry creates. Postliberals have demonstrated several classical techniques in their teaching with the aim of creating surprise. Indeed, Harvey illustrates how students in his organisation dynamics classes produce written poetry, sing theories, make movies, cook concepts, and literally juggle constructs (1979).

Other pedagogical approaches which have leveraged Greek and Roman classical traditions for focusing on student being include the efforts of Byrne and colleagues (2018) to engage in a process of self-awareness intended to lead an individual to proactively develop their character. For the authors, self-awareness of one's own virtue is prompted by 'crucible moments – transformative experiences through which individuals come to a new or altered sense of identity' (Byrne et al., 2018, p.265). Such situations are important because they require an individual to make sense of challenging moments and adverse situations. To present students with a crucible learning experience, the authors engage their students in a five-day course with current and former members of the Canadian Armed Forces. This learning involved physical challenges, team tasks, and reflection exercises.

However, the challenge in a modern university context is often around finding pedagogical space to encourage the surfacing of student character. There are challenges in replicating a five-day off-campus experience, and common pedagogical techniques such as movies and guest speakers are unlikely to draw a formative response from students (Taylor, 2018). However, Hibbert and colleagues (2018) present a perhaps more manageable pedagogy for student formation by leveraging aesthetic experiences such as art, which engage the whole person. Defining formation as 'a holistic process of being formed' (Hibbert et al., 2018, p.604), the authors set out a process which involves the experience of interpretation, the role of dialogue, and the interpretation of experience to improve a person's long-term accumulation of insights and judgement.

Because art defies categorisation, it engages the individual in unpredictable ways and allows them to learn and grow. Similarly, dialogue is important to formation because we can only understand ourselves in a relational context. Through exploring similarities and differences with others, dialogue assists the individual in development of moral character and virtues such as altruism and humility. Finally, formation occurs through interpretation of experience rooted in a struggle to understand rather than resolve. Here, different histories and traditions are important for sensemaking efforts related to our experience, our past, and the larger context in which we live. Through outlining this process, Hibbert and colleagues put forward pedagogies involving art, tradition, and dialogue for enabling students to engage in their own personal formation.

In adopting this underlying emphasis on phronesis, Postliberals shy away from the Rational School interest in models and frameworks and instead focus on how individuals engage in acts of personal meaning. The position is articulated by Akin (2000) that more facts and greater precision are unlikely to provide better understanding of work. Rather, gains are to be made from 'producing more evocative stories and rich images that will show what work is like', where the job of the management educator is to 'create artful portrayals and interpretations' (Akin, 2000, p.58).

An example of this story-based approach is provided by Akin (1995) in his consulting project at a factory in a semi-rural southern US town. Called in by management to address what they perceived as a lack of teamwork in the factory, Akin quickly found his academic language was too remote from worker practice to enable them to make sense of what they were doing. 'There wasn't much richness when talking about teamwork, and there wasn't much to be heard when people were actually working, as they were merely "doing their job". It was all suffused with a kind of banality that belied the actual accomplishments and flattened the experience' (Akin, 1995, p.490). Akin's solution was to encourage deeper interpersonal relationships through a lexicon he developed around NASCAR racing, a shared area of interest between managers and workers.

Because the intention of the Postliberal educator is to adopt pedagogies and techniques which will help students understand themselves, they reject the tag of teacher. This situation is addressed from a management education perspective by Jerry Harvey in his opinion piece 'Learning To Not Teach' (1979). Harvey presents a view of the professor as a learner. Harvey charges management educators with an overriding focus on teaching rather than learning. He reflects on learning as a more difficult educational ambition because 'it involves essence', and therefore dismisses teaching as founded on an 'illusion that the power to grow lies with someone else [other than the student]' (Harvey, 1979, p.19).

In a later piece, Harvey reinforces the case against teachers. He argues that any understanding of education which relies on a definition that the student is taught means therefore that student learning should be credited to the teacher. Criticising this perspective, Harvey puts forward the argument that this view violates the essence of the student and reduces them to an 'inanimate, passive receptacle' (Harvey, 1999, p.76). The Postliberal response is therefore that organising principles for the management educator should be on the inner frame of reference of the actor (Vaill, 1984).

The issue of teaching versus learning is further explored by Vaill (1981) in a cryptic piece called 'Exploration and Discovery'. As a metaphorical precursor to his later work on white water learning, Vaill teases at the learning experience by creating a fictional conversation between a person pursuing a typical teacher–student model of interaction, and around-the-world sailor Francis Chichester. The person starts off by interrogating Chichester on what they should be getting out of a learning experience. Chichester responds with puzzlement, to which the person replies by flattering the sailor and attempting the same question again in a different way. Chichester then provides a Postliberal response by dissuading the person from the notion that he is a teacher, 'you have a theory of me as a person-with-a-key' (Vaill, 1981, p.16). The sailor tries to turn the frame of reference back on the student themself by emphasising that progress in any pursuit is about the individual's own ability to cope with confusion and uncertainty. In a nod to phronesis, Chichester argues that the only way to learn and grow is to 'correct course every day' (Vaill, 1981, p.16).

An example of how the educator–student dynamic plays out in a Postliberal management education classroom is outlined by Sparks (forthcoming) in his illustration of his mid-1990s experiences in Jerry Harvey's *Organization Dynamics* classes. Sparks recounts that Harvey entered the first class and asked students, 'why are we here?' When the responses were on his book and other questions around his teaching, Harvey exited the room and didn't return.

This situation replayed in the second week of the course, where Harvey shut the door a little louder on his exit. It was only in the third week when a student asked Harvey, 'why are you doing this to us?', that he outlined his learning approach and sought to draw out the frustration, anxiety, and irritation that the students' expectations of a professorial sage had created. Sparks reflects on the impact this approach had on the being of the students, 'we would be evaluated on our ability to learn and grow in this class that was more of an experimental lab than a traditional class' (Sparks, forthcoming).

The Postliberal approach has seen several medieval court and ancient Greek and Roman metaphors deployed to characterise the management educator. Akin (1995) describes the educational role as that of minstrel. Denis Pym has been described in his obituary as a holy fool or court jester (Shipley, 2019). Dent's tribute to the careers of Postliberal educators Peter Vaill and Jerry Harvey leverages descriptors including student of the people, or heretic (2002). On the separate passing of both men in subsequent years, Dent follows up by describing Vaill as poet laureate (2022), while his tribute to Harvey describes him as a timeless seer (2017). Such descriptors capture a paradoxical understanding of the educator role. A piece by Clegg and colleagues on the court jester might equally apply across these other court roles, in that such positions are intended to 'mitigate the excesses of power, while serving and supporting the ruler through a license to jest' (Clegg et al., 2022).

To provide a portrait of the foolish management educator, we turn to Birkbeck University of London's obituary to Professor Denis Pym on his passing in 2019. Noting his informal and irreverent Australian manner, the tribute praises Pym for being:

> a notably good listener, treating people as equals. He was uninterested in status, reputation and financial rewards for himself, preferring to be identified professionally as author, critic and editor, rather than use academic titles. He saw himself as enacting the role of the holy fool, or licensed court jester allowed to whisper in the ear of the medieval king warning him of the trap set by hubris … providing a practical example of dignified work in the local economy, where individuals are enabled to recover self-respect, reclaiming some lost authority through self-employment and warm meaningful relationships in the community. (Shipley, 2019)

The obituary notes Pym's legacy in planting thousands of trees, and his efforts in freely providing labour to those in his local village who required assistance. The tribute concludes, 'a deep thinker, Denis Pym wanted us to wake from our slumbers, from the abuse of modern technology and other forms of abuse, to take back responsibility, our autonomy, and believe in ourselves, our capacity to add to the common good' (Shipley, 2019). It is this notion of the common good which provides the basis for a virtue ethics approach to Postliberal management education.

UNDERSTANDING HOW EVERYONE BEHAVES

The foolish educator works towards a sense of a shared common humanity. In so doing, Postliberals reject the consequentialist and rights-based ethical approaches of the Rational and Critical schools which they believe are anchored in individualism. Indeed, Postliberals contend it is not possible for either the Rational or Critical schools to present an ethical position because they have moved away from an understanding of the world based on meta-physical transcendence, to one informed by rational immanence (Del Noce & Lancellotti, 2015).

The Postliberal case against consequentialist and rights-based ethical philosophies is traced by Carlin (2021b), in providing a lineage from ancient Gnosticism to current attempts to produce an ethical academy. Gnostics emerged in Greece in the first and second century as a breakaway from Christianity. The starting point of Gnostic perspectives is inherently anti-Christian. It holds a view there are two worlds, and humans are impris-oned in a lesser world which is positively evil (Perrin, 1974). For Gnostics, the hope was for a saviour who would come into this irredeemably evil world and offer humans knowledge of the way to escape out of the darkness and into the light of the second world. Here then is evident the lineage to the Critical school and its emancipatory ambitions through a long-standing Gnostic philosophy which combines radical dualism with a despair of the world. However, where Gnostics preserve the metaphysical notion of a saviour who might redeem this evil world, contemporary Critical scholars cast aside the supernatural in favour of an atheism where the power resides in man to radically transform the world (Carlin, 2021b).

Carlin distinguishes ancient gnosis where redemption is only possible in the afterlife, from contemporary liberalism where the descendants of Gnosticism 'believe that self-redemption is possible in this world through the enactment of specifically formulated projects of social engineering tied to unquestionable truths, and an irrefutable cognitive mastery of the world' (2021b, pp.438–439). Postliberals tie this new liberal Gnosticism to the elimination of any shared set of values on what constitutes the good. Replaced by relativistic ethics based on being yourself, the liberal cause rejects all claims of objective and univer-sal truth. For Postliberals, the elimination of shared value means that ethics become commensurable with power.

> Even when absolute values such as 'social justice' and 'equity' are promoted in universities, they are ultimately limited in function and scope. While implicitly posited as transcendental, these concepts can only be mobilized by those specific individuals/groups who are most effectively able to politicize them in their favour. (Carlin, 2021b, p.442)

While management education is yet to provide such a direct challenge to consequentialist and rights-based ethics, there is some work which presents a sceptical take on underlying Rational and Critical frameworks. For example, Hennessey (1980, p.3) laments a relativistic attitude of 'it all depends', when it comes to the issue of values in teaching.

Meanwhile King (1983) explores distinctions between the liberal emphasis on individual rights, as derived from Thomas Hobbes, John Locke, and Adam Smith, from the duty to others inherent to Plato, Aristotle, and Thomas Aquinas. King argues that the liberal move towards individual rights has changed the context of ethical decision making, away from local institutions such as the family, and towards global entities such as the corporation. In prosecuting this case, King quotes noted Harvard University post-industrial theorist Daniel Bell:

> To the extent that the traditional sources of social support (the small town, church, and family), have crumbled in society, new kinds of organizations, particularly the corporation, have taken their place; and these inevitably become the arenas in which the demands for security, justice, and esteem are made. To think of the business corporation, then, simply as an economic instrument is to fail totally to understand the meaning of the social changes of the last half century. (Bell, 1971, p.5)

In a follow-up piece, King (1984) introduces MacIntyre to the management education literature. MacIntyre's (1981) work *After Virtue* is considered a classic in the field of political philosophy for its attempt at reviving older forms of Aristotelian moral philosophy. Critical of social sciences for its absence of law-like generalisations, King leverages MacIntyre's insights in critiquing what he perceives as an emerging relativistic philosophical position that no scientific choice can be made between ultimate values. MacIntyre argues that such a position must lead to a 'bureaucratic individualism' where centralised authority of government and corporations works against local associations and social groups to create a pluralist politics in danger of devolving into states of near anarchy (in King, 1984).

For Postliberals, the response to the individualism which pervades both Rational and Critical School approaches to management education lies in a return to ancient Greek and Roman ethical traditions set against the context of experience and a shared vision of what is right and moral. If no such shared sense of vision is enacted, people perceive their lives to be a 'dead end street' and 'their stories have no coherence' (King, 1984, p.24). King therefore presents a call for a return to universalisms inherent to virtuous behaviours of courage, honesty, and justice as providing the moral foundation for persons to experience shared meaning in their daily lives.

Several management educators have subsequently continued this classical approach towards their calling. In a discussion on MBA education, Duncan

(1986) leverages the Greek concept of *telos*, meaning the purpose and goal of life and work, to consider what should be the ultimate responsibility of an MBA programme. Critical of the results-oriented nature of MBA proponents to focus on the outcomes of study as a career 'fast track', Duncan argues that the results of such thinking have been an educational homogeneity. In a move which seems to foretell of the MBA's role in the Enron and Global Financial Crisis scandals of ensuing decades, Duncan argues that Executive Education must move beyond results thinking of profits. He suggests instead a *telos* where managers are encouraged to 'courageously reject the prescriptions of the models [they learn] on the basis of a higher duty than simply to optimize a set of factors, or to ponder the ultimate wisdom of one's behavior under conditions of risk' (1986, p.72).

In a subsequent piece on the teaching of ethics in business schools, Jones (1989) argues the need for a management education which focuses on the development of a student's moral character, or virtue. Individual character and personal ideals are essential to ethical deliberations and must therefore be taught by example. This means that the teacher should focus on their own moral development by engaging in a practice of 'moral introspection and reflectiveness', for providing an exemplar for students to follow (Jones, 1989, p.8).

This notion of presenting a model of exemplary behaviour is further pursued by Brady (1990), who argues that the educator should display respectful inter-action with students, staff, and colleagues. Continuing the Postliberal theme of learning versus teaching, the author considers the most appropriate role for the management educator to adopt in conducting courses on business ethics. Posing the question as to whether ethics educators should be detached intel-lectuals or moral activists, Brady sets out a case against the moral activist. He suggests that activist educators are likely to introduce controversy into experi-ential pedagogical techniques which might then create fallout by eliciting per-sonal revelations about students and deliberately provoking confrontation. In contrast, the educator who remains more detached is likely to provide 'the best lessons in ethics', by modelling 'fairness, equity, diligence, respectfulness, and reasonability' (Brady, 1990, p.26).

While topics of virtue and character remained relatively unexplored in management education for the rest of the 1990s, the wider ethical turn asso-ciated with the collapse of Enron, Arthur Andersen, and Morgan Stanley has prompted several authors to return to these themes. Hartman (2006) contem-plates an understanding of moral behaviour as anchored in a person's charac-ter, including their virtues and vices. Leveraging insights from Aristotle, the author argues that humans have certain enduring desires which provide good reason to act in a certain manner. For example, someone of generous character will see people around them in need and feel compelled to help. Hartman suggests that the role of management education is to help students think critically about their values and realise them in practice. Consistent with the Postliberal School, Aristotelian virtue ethics 'takes status in the community seriously, does not presuppose equality as a good, and deemphasizes rights' (Hartman, 2006, p.70). The author's suggestion is for case studies and literature directed at encouraging students to reflect on their own values, so that when a moral situation arises in future employment, they may recognise the stakes.

Halliday and Johnsson (2009) take up similar themes by re-engaging with MacIntyre's virtue ethics to consider the issue of learning in organisations. Speculating that organisations can be economically efficient while maintaining cultures built around empathy, kindness, and decency, the authors discuss the notion of communities of practice. Their argument is that for such bodies to be ethical in the MacIntyrian sense they must be built on relational dependencies which ask what is best for the group to do. The piece concludes that a focus on mission statements and power is unlikely to be sufficient for creating an ethical organisation, and that a concern for virtue is necessary for bringing a moral dimension to organisational learning.

In the pursuit of an education based on character and virtue, one challenge for Postliberals in a secular world is the extent to which spirituality should be embedded in the management education curricula. Identifying the relevance of spirituality to a range of topics such as leadership, the meaning of work, ethics, and connectedness, Crossman (2015) leverages discussion with business managers to speculate on techniques for embedding spirituality within the management education context. These include giving space for students to develop self-awareness and reflection on spiritual issues, and for the educator to use their voice to speak with spirituality. To illustrate the manner in which the foolish teacher can bring spirituality into their classroom approach, Crossman leverages the example of pioneering management researcher and Jesuit educator André Delbecq (2000), who speaks 'in the voice of his own Catholic tradition, remaining respectful to others that exist and are shared in the learning space' (Crossman, 2015, p.376).

In terms of operationalising a Postliberal management education on ethics, Eriksen and colleagues (2019) introduce a practical pedagogy for encouraging students to develop their own virtue. Seeking to move beyond personal reflection and compliance-driven educational methods, the authors develop an internally driven, practice-focused, values-based approach to student learning about ethics. The authors first introduce students to the virtues of temperance, silence, order, resolution, frugality, industry, sincerity, justice, modernisation, cleanliness, tranquillity, chastity, and humility. Working on Aristotle's view that it is necessary to learn virtues through deliberate practice, one of the authors develops an assignment whereby students identify four virtues they wish to cultivate, and focus on living one of these virtues over a four-week period. As this process unfolds, students engage in weekly discussions about their experiences of learning and development associated with the assignment, and at the end of the assignment they are prompted to respond to questions for reflecting on what they had learned about themselves. Subsequent surveys show that students believe the assignment allows them to improve behaviours consistent with their chosen virtues and increase their self-understanding and self-reflection (Eriksen et al., 2019).

Comer and Schwartz (2020) provide a different pedagogy for character development by introducing the Jewish spiritual practice of *Mussar*. Consistent with the Postliberal tradition, *Mussar* recognises the limits of human nature by acknowledging character deficiencies and excesses. The authors leverage *Mussar* to set out a process of becoming more virtuous by engaging in reflection, setting goals, monitoring progress, and making adjustments. Drawing on critiques of business ethics education as having had minimal impact on executive behaviour (Simha et al., 2012), Comer and Shwartz introduce a *Mussar*-inspired teaching practice for increasing student awareness of individual character, providing a basic vocabulary of character traits, helping students identify the character traits they would like to address, and providing them with a process for self-enhancement of their character.

Focusing on 24 character traits including compassion, courage, diligence (responsibility), honesty, forgiveness, and humility, Comer and Schwartz outline a classroom approach where they encourage student learning of the character traits, and then ask them to undertake self-reflection. Students consider their behaviour over a one-week period, and then submit daily logs to reflect on any character deficiencies or excesses as they experience difficult encounters or decisions. Students use this reflective work to identify two character traits they would most like to change and develop a relevant goal worksheet for working towards this change. Over the next week, students track their progress and submit a four- or five-sentence report on whether they have attained their goal.

In conclusion, the Postliberal approach to ethics rejects the relativistic rights-based framework on which Critical education is based. Instead, Postliberals advocate a return to Greek and Roman traditions of a virtue- and character-based ethics and apply pedagogical techniques based on reflection and practice for drawing out student understanding of themselves and their strengths and weaknesses. In adopting this approach, the foolish educator advances the position that ours is a shared humanity, where the virtues and vices inherent to the character of one person are reflected across all of us. It is this commonality of character which drives the Postliberal approach to identity in education of a search for similarity.

SEARCHING FOR SIMILARITY

The Postliberal rejection of relativist rights-based ethics provides for a cynicism around Critical notions of caring and the push for an understanding of identity based in concern for that which is shared. This position is reflected by Pym:

> I do believe that the elevation of human dignity must be the overriding and continuing concern of any social enquiry. This disposition is different, I hope, from the 'caring, sharing, wanting to help others' phoney humanism that is currently riding high. Behind such apparently noble causes lie coercive games and the reducing effects of bureaucratized welfare and proceduralized democracy. (Pym, 1990, p.235)

The Postliberal push for an understanding of identity grounded in common humanity is perhaps best illustrated by Wendell Berry in his essay, *The Hidden Wound* (2010). Tackling the complex issue of race in the United States, Berry sets out his own family's history with slavery. Born to a white, tobacco farming family in Kentucky, Berry recounts growing up with two Black employees, and how his invitation as a child to one of them to his birthday party caused division within his family. Because his invitee was not welcome by some of the white guests, Berry recounts how he was forced to stay outside the house during his own party. He uses this experience as a prompt for researching his family's history with slavery, focusing on his great-grandfather's decision to sell an 'unmanageable' slave. Berry concludes that slavery represents violence. 'The violence was systemic, and every slave owner complicit. Even a master who did not want to use cruelty had to exercise at least the cruelty of abandonment: selling the slave into cruelty somewhere else' (Hochschild, 2020).

Consistent with the Postliberal tradition, Berry searches for a unifying element in the story of slavery. His conclusion is that by perpetuating such violence on Black people, whites have created in themselves a self-inflicted, hidden wound. 'As the oppressors they [whites] feel, secretly or otherwise, morally inferior to those they have oppressed' (Berry, 2010, p.92).

In search of a way of bringing the races together, Berry works through literary classics including *The Odyssey* (Homer, 1919), *The Adventures of Huckleberry Finn* (Twain, 2010), and *War and Peace* (Tolstoy, 1993), to conclude that strength, dignity, and joy can only come from the grace of a person's human bonds and their sense of belonging to the land. Here, Berry perceives the white man as remaining morally adrift because he has become divorced from this sense of belonging to the land, instead living in cities, and viewing the country only as a resource to be exploited through machines and corporations.

Berry argues, 'empowered by technology, the abstractions of the white man's domination of the continent threaten now to annihilate the specific characteristics of all races, virtues and vices alike, absorbing them as neutral components into a machine society' (Berry, 2018, p.107). Leveraging this insight, Berry continues towards the defining feature of his common humanity, the recognition of human power.

> It is, then, not simply a question of Black power or white power, but of how meaningfully to reenfranchise human power. This, as I think Martin Luther King understood, is the real point, the real gift to America, or the struggle of the Black people. In accepting the humanity of the Black race, the white race will not be giving accommodation to an alien people; it will be receiving into itself half of its own experience, vital and indispensable to it, which it has so far denied at great cost. (Berry, 2018, p.107)

In this search for commonality, the aim of the foolish educator is to build community through character. This position is made possible by the essentialist nature of Aristotelian virtue, where what is good for one person will be good for others too. 'Since human beings are social creatures, the good life, hence good character, involves living satisfactorily in a congenial community. So your virtues cause you to benefit your family and friend and people in your community' (Hartman, 2006, p.70).

For management educators, the position of fostering community through good character is taken up by Harvey. In a piece likely to be considered controversial by many educators today, Harvey (1984) encourages students to cheat. Starting out with the provocation, 'as a professor of organization behavior I have long believed that I have an ethical responsibility to encourage students in my class to cheat' (Harvey, 1984, p.1), the author sets out the case that by defining cheating as the act of helping or being helped by others, the Academy has taken the virtuous act of altruism and mischaracterised it as immoral and dishonourable. To the Postliberal, this pursuit of individualism over community is familiar.

Harvey considers the negative effects of standard definitions of cheating based around copying works of other students. To do so, he couches his provocation in Postliberal positions on the importance of community and the rejection of individual moral relativism. First, he argues that contemporary approaches to cheating condemn the struggling student to the risk of anaclitic depression. This form of depression occurs when a person has their emotional support taken away by thwarting their needs for community and engagement. Second, Harvey contends that typical cheating definitions prevent students from expressing altruism, the process of 'getting pleasure from giving others what you yourself would like to receive' (Valliant, 1977, p.11). According to this view, Harvey perceives the Academy as removing a 'transcendental quality that distinguishes human beings from animals ... and is a requirement for the survival of any culture' (Harvey, 1984, p.3). Third, Harvey prosecutes the case that standard cheating definitions thwart the expression of synergy by undermining the understanding that many individuals perform their best when working with others. Finally, Harvey contends that the standard definition of cheating does not reflect how work is performed in organisations. He argues that managers spend little time working alone, and employees regularly receive aid from their colleagues in order to complete work of a satisfactory standard.

To put in place an academic system which encourages community and rejects individualism, Harvey redefines cheating as the failure to assist others when they request it. He sets this out in his class syllabus as follows:

> You may take the examination alone, with another person, or with as many other people as you would like. I frown on cheating. In fact, I go blind with rage if I catch anyone cheating. I define cheating as the failure to assist others on the examination if they request it. (Harvey, 1984, p.6)

Reflecting on his approach, Harvey found that students were largely welcoming of his new definition of cheating, while faculty often responded with hostility. He reports one colleague as saying, 'Professor Harvey, what are you trying to do? Infect the brains of our young people with immoral, communistic thoughts? It's your kind of thinking that led to the demise of the Roman Empire' (Harvey, 1984, p.7). Harvey concludes that the standard definition of cheating is 'unethical, immoral, destructive, and in its own way, evil; for I believe the suppression of altruism in ourselves and others for the purpose of enhancing or maintaining our personal power is always an expression of the darkness of our souls' (Harvey, 1984, p.8). It is not unreasonable to imagine that Harvey would have seen the subsequent rise of plagiarism mills and essay writing artificial intelligence (AI) technology as natural outcomes of the Academy's standard approach to cheating.

The intent of Harvey's work on cheating is to build a Postliberal communitarian mindset in students. Its impact is illustrated by Eleni Stavrou, a Harvey student. In reflecting from a contemporary viewpoint on Harvey's work on cheating, the author draws a line between standard academic definitions of cheating and the behaviour of executives in the world of finance to favour personal gains over client interests. Capturing Harvey's educational focus on human essence, Stavrou argues 'he had a significant impact in my education, my subsequent career and, most importantly, my character' (2017, p.124). Stavrou explains that in going against the grain to redefine cheating and express the importance of altruism, her mentor had assisted in clarifying her guiding values in life and provided long-lasting effects on both her mind and heart.

The role of the educator is important in providing the conditions under which students can search for similarity with others. Again, a student illustration of Harvey is illuminating. Sparks' (2017) 'My "F" in Life: A Tribute to Jerry B. Harvey' outlines how an educator might create conditions for drawing out student character. The story takes place in the context of an assignment on small group behaviour and change. While Sparks' peers took up Harvey's challenge to complete the assignment by creatively writing poems and performing songs, Sparks declares he felt insecure at this prospect. Instead, he chose to produce a written assessment focused on the very personal story of his pending divorce, and the dysfunction of dependency.

Harvey's first step in drawing out Sparks' character is to call the student to his office to receive his grade. The professor then prompts the student with a probing question on why he has been called to his office. Sparks recalls presenting a series of answers which failed to impress Harvey, before finally offering the view that he was there to talk about his divorce. Harvey then turns the focus to helping Sparks understand himself, 'I'll give you a B- on that response son, we're here to talk about you' (Sparks, 2017, p.119).

Leveraging the Postliberal focus on story, Harvey encourages Sparks to detail circumstances behind his marriage breakdown. On hearing the student's view, Harvey first attempts to build a shared humanity by offering his sorrow on the circumstances of the marriage breakdown and declaring he would pray for both Sparks and his soon-to-be ex-wife. Sparks notes that Harvey always held a personal objection to feedback, which he believed was grounded in a philosophical human materialism that encouraged participants to treat each other as objects. Therefore, in a Postliberal nod to a metaphysical order, praying together with his student was Harvey's preferred approach.

Following on from the prayer, Harvey provides Sparks with an 'A' grade on the paper for knowing the subject matter around concepts of dysfunction and dependency. However, distinguishing between the Rational School's emphasis on skills and becoming with the Postliberal School's weight on character and being, Harvey then provides Sparks with some bad news. 'I'm giving you an "F" in life' (Sparks, 2017, p.120). Harvey asserts that Sparks had created a dynamic in his marriage in which he always had to be right and where he had to solve every problem. 'You want me to feel sorry for you, but I don't. Not at all. I feel sorry for her' (Sparks, 2017, p.120). Keeping with the tone of personal formation, Harvey's suggestion to Sparks is that he should spend the next four years at George Washington University working out why he had created this situation in his marriage.

The example provided by Sparks suggests techniques the foolish educator might use to focus on student character. These approaches include using a different setting (Harvey's office) to help students reflect, a probing question to draw the student's attention inward, the offer of sympathy and support to leverage a deeper commonality between student and teacher, and finally a suggestion of a path for ongoing personal formation.

One key component of any course where student being is the focus is for the educator to set in place boundaries which include space for guided personal reflection. Reflection is required throughout the duration of a course (rather than at the end) and should be directed at improving the student's self-awareness (Roberts, 2008). Yet, reflection is not an easy practice to master. Management guru, Henry Mintzberg has weighed in on this topic, and even likens the practice to the Christian notion of struggle. 'Reflection does not mean musing, and it is not casual. It means wondering, probing, analyzing, synthesizing, connecting' (2004, p.254).

Self-reflection, learning to build one's self awareness, is important to developing a student's own insights on their beliefs and assumptions. Questions such as 'what am I learning about myself as I learn about the subject?' can be useful in helping the student explore their own behaviours and thoughts (Hedberg, 2009, p.15). Modelling reflective behaviour is an important role for the management educator. Hedberg outlines a process of asking aloud how a particular activity is going, or adding her own observations about an activity as students engage in it. Through such a process, we see a common Postliberal practice. Through self-awareness, the student is guided towards an understanding of what they share in common with others. In the Postliberal School, individuality therefore becomes a basis for community.

CONCLUSION

Overall, we can see how the Postliberal School presents in management education. By ignoring production, foolish educators reject the educational approach on the student becoming favoured by Rational and Critical scholars, to instead help students understand themselves. In so doing, they reject the activist role of the rebel teacher, even stepping away from the idea of being a teacher to the point where they resemble heretics and other medieval court characters in attempting to speak truth to power. Their rejection of the moral relativism of the Critical School means that Postliberals develop an approach to ethics in education which is based on a return to Greek and Roman classical works for developing a shared humanity built around virtue. In so doing, foolish educators reject the individualist leanings of Rational and Critical approaches to identity, and instead seek techniques for building virtues such as altruism.

The Postliberal School is the final one of the three management education schools to be outlined in this book. We have now seen how the Rational, Critical, and Postliberal schools have evolved over time, and the underlying relations to the organisation implicated by each approach. Leveraging this information, it is therefore possible to speculate on what the development of these schools to date might mean for the future of management education research.

QUESTIONS FOR THE READER

1. Quickly write down your three immediate takes on the foundations of the Postliberal School. Do these foundations match your own beliefs and values on management education?
2. What is your position on knowledge in social science? Do you consider it to be a scientific endeavour? Or do you think there are things which are unknowable?
3. Do you think of yourself as a teacher or a learner?
4. What is your position on an educational dichotomy of becoming versus being? Are we unlimited individuals who can become whatever we want? Or are we beings who are more limited by our own virtues and vices?
5. If you were to develop a reflective student curriculum that encourages them to focus on their own character, how might it look? Around which topics in your course would you embed such learning?
6. Can you see a link between standard definitions of student cheating and the rise of plagiarism windmills and assignments produced by AI? Taken in the light of such consideration, what do you think of Harvey's redefinition of cheating as a form of altruism?
7. Considering Harvey's definition of cheating, might there be ways you could change your teaching practice around student assignments to incorporate a more altruistic approach to assessment?

6. Advancing the future of management education research

Given the premise of this book, that the best way to advance the future of management education research is through developing academics who take a fascination in the field, this final chapter offers a variety of study topics which researchers might seek to explore in pursuing their own work. Returning to Bourdieu's (1969) understanding of an intellectual field as comprising institutions, practices, social relations, and beliefs, the intent is to introduce a series of interesting questions around these aspects of the field of management education on which emerging and existing scholars might found their work.

Earlier chapters have outlined beliefs and practices associated with the Rational, Critical, and Postliberal schools of management education. As a recap, the worlds of the three schools are underpinned by a range of foundational beliefs based on different philosophies, ethics, motivations, and notions of authority. These beliefs result in a variety of practical manifestations, including images of the teacher and educational intents. To assist the reader in piecing together their journey through the different worlds of management education, Table 6.1 presents a summary comparison of the underlying beliefs and practices of the three schools.

To recap, the Rational School is established in an American tradition of rational pragmatism and evolutionary consequentialism found in the works of philosophers such as Peirce (1878, 1901), James (1922), and Dewey (1922, 1929). The Rational School approach is of knowledge through action. Hence, the meaning of a particular subject comes about via the meaning it attains through practice. In taking the view there can be positive aspects to authority, the image of the teacher in the Rational School is of a tinkerer always trying to improve the educational experience. Motivated by an intent to build student skills for entering the workforce, tinkerers deploy pedagogies for improving soft and hard skills, teaching their students how to behave in the workplace, and embracing equality.

Meanwhile, the Critical School is founded in a radical poststructuralism associated with European philosophers such as Fromm (1941), Foucault (1977), and Marcuse (1968), and a moral relativism associated with Rawls (1971). Based on an opposition to the totalitarian forces which emerged in World War II, the position of the Critical scholar is to flee from authority.

Table 6.1   The worlds of the three schools of management education

	Foundational beliefs		
	Rational School	Critical School	Postliberal School
Philosophy	Rational pragmatism	Radical poststructuralism	Divine metaphysics
Ethics	Evolutionary consequentialism	Moral relativism	Virtue ethics
Motivation	Embrace of the liberal	Opposition to the totalitarian	Affinity with the traditional
Notion of authority	Authority as freedom to	Authority as freedom from	Authority as freedom to
	Practical manifestations		
Image of the teacher	Tinkerer	Rebel	Fool
Educational intent	Building student skills	Emancipating the student	Forming student being
Organisational skills	Improving hard and soft skills	Disrupting corporate production	Forming the self
Workplace behaviour	Understanding how to behave	Understanding how others behave	Understanding how everyone behaves
Approach to the individual	Embracing equality	Pushing for equity	Searching for similarity

Hence, the motivation of founding Critical educators such as Freire (1972) is to emancipate students from oppressive western power structures. Educators in this school take on the image of a rebel in pursuing pedagogical techniques for disrupting corporate production, understanding how others behave, and pushing for equity of the marginalised and oppressed.

Finally, the Postliberal School is established in a divine metaphysics and virtue ethics associated with classical scholars such as Aristotle, C.S. Lewis (1975), and Del Noce (Del Noce & Lancellotti, 2015). Based on an understanding of authority as the capability to make grow, Postliberals perceive value in collective traditional institutions such as the family, church, community, and the nation. The motivation of Postliberal educators such as Harvey (1979) and Vaill (1996) is to establish conditions for forming student being. Educators in this school have been metaphorically likened here to the fool, as they leverage pedagogies for forming the self, understanding how everyone behaves, and searching for a deeper common humanity.

To bring these insights together on the three schools and suggest future possible topics of study, we now turn our attention to how social relations between the schools and the institutions of the scholarly journals on which they are based have changed over time.

INSTITUTIONS AND SOCIAL RELATIONS IN THE INTELLECTUAL FIELD OF MANAGEMENT EDUCATION: WHERE ARE WE NOW?

To consider social relations between the three schools, a snapshot is provided on how they appear to have ebbed and flowed over time. To complete this undertaking, the work reflects on the institutions that represent the three leading journals, *Management Learning* (ML), *Journal of Management Education* (JME), and *Academy of Management Learning and Education* (AMLE). It should be noted that the following is illustrative, rather than a formal bibliometric analysis. There are no formal quantitative counts of articles. Instead, this snapshot is based on the themes identified in the earlier chapters on each of the three schools and how they appear to have emerged in the post-1970 period.

From the 1970s, to the start of the Millennium, the Rational School seems to have been the ascendant approach to management education. Emerging from the notion that management education is a national project of providing skills for industry (Gordon & Howell, 1959; Pierson, 1959), the Rational School is mainly reflected in the post-1975 period in the pages of JME, where topics on preparing students for the workplace through pragmatic pedagogies have achieved prominence. Hence, the focus on both hard technological skills (e.g. Hope & Higgins, 1985), and soft skills in empathy and communication (e.g. Powers, 1975). At a similar time, management education literature also engaged in debate on the ethical role of teachers. Should they be detached intellectuals or moral activists when it came to matters of ethics in the classroom (Brady, 1990)? Meanwhile the approach to identity evolved from helping white males manage women and racial minorities in the workforce (e.g. Seashore, 1976), to one where more substantive efforts at developing women into leadership positions were pursued (e.g. Cunningham, 1981).

During this pre-Millennium period, movements in Critical and Postliberal management education were fledgling. Critical scholarship leveraged the pages of ML and seized on corporate disasters such as Bhopal and the Exxon Valdez oil spill to advance the notion of power as a negative and often unconscious concept (e.g. Tosey, 1989), while pursuing an ethics of standing up for the marginalised and oppressed (e.g. Snell, 1986, 1989). These Critical scholars acted in advance of the Rational School on matters of racial and sexual identity to progress workplace issues related to women (e.g. Fonda, 1979) and people of colour (e.g. Jones, 1994). Meanwhile, Postliberals used occasional dispatches in JME to advance an understanding of a limited human being (e.g.

Athos, 1979), advocate for a return to virtue ethics (e.g. King, 1984), and seek the togetherness inherent to virtues such as altruism (e.g. Harvey, 1984).

The Millennium appears to have brought with it a Critical turn in management education. The collapse of Enron and misdeeds of Arthur Andersen seem to have been seminal events for the field. Their basis in the unethical acts of managers who had been educated in leading business schools has prompted a deep introspection. In its wake, Rational scholarship has been accused of marginalising issues of morality (e.g. Ghoshal, 2005). This leads to themes which establish pushback against western features of management education for being unethical, including textbooks (e.g. Mir, 2003), masculinity (e.g. Dobson & White, 1995), and even the business school itself (e.g. Jones et al., 2020). However, the move also heralds a shift to human-centred worldviews of pluralist ethics (e.g. Giacalone & Thompson, 2006), and a push for equity in standing up for marginalised racial (e.g. Macalpine & Marsh, 2005) and sexual identities (e.g. Rudin et al., 2016).

The establishment of the United Nations Principles for Responsible Management Education (PRME) has also induced Rational scholarship towards an understanding of an ethical role to play for the educator (e.g. Forray & Leigh, 2012), while a more activist position that the teacher should advocate for positive social change now features as a standard call in the main journals (e.g. Greenberg & Hibbert, 2022). The result of these shifts appears to be a breaking down of distinctions between the Rational and Critical schools in the areas of ethics and identity. Meanwhile, Postliberal scholarship continues to be seldom published, though there are occasional pieces which push the cause of virtue ethics (Eriksen et al., 2019) and recognise the limits of human nature (Comer & Schwartz, 2020).

In providing this brief snapshot of the intellectual field, several questions emerge. What does this trajectory of development mean for scholars in the field? And what might the terrain of that which has been covered in scholarship to this point suggest for the future of management education research? Each of the three schools poses questions of the other schools, especially the Critical and Postliberal schools, where the more Critical nature of scholarship casts uncertainty on other approaches to management education. In this final section, we turn to the beliefs, practices, institutions, and social relations of the intellectual field, to suggest questions that emerging scholars may find intellectually profitable to investigate in advancing the future of management education research.

QUESTIONS ON BELIEFS IN THE INTELLECTUAL FIELD OF MANAGEMENT EDUCATION

The preceding work in this book identifies a number of questions which scholars may like to pose on underlying beliefs of the schools. It is suggested there are grounds to investigate the empirical basis of the Rational School, the radical nature and approach to authority of the Critical School, and the traditional nature of the Postliberal School.

As outlined in the chapter on the Rational School, its philosophical basis in rational pragmatism makes for an uneasy empiricism. Peirce, James, and Dewey represent a tradition which is by no means wholly consistent with a scientific empirical tradition (Joullie & Spillane, 2020). Indeed, their position is similar to that of the Postliberal School, in casting doubt on social science which seems to look like that of a natural science. For the Rational scholar, a starting point on investigations along these lines may be found in King (1984), who takes issue with what he perceives as the habit of social science to focus on the empirical side of social theory to the detriment of its interpretive and normative components. This means an over-reliance on an analytical justification for decisions, while ignoring its normative moral dimension. Here, he quotes public intellectual Irving Kristol on sociology as a body of knowledge which does 'not have the status of scientific truths' (in King, 1984, p.15).

There appears a prime opportunity for Rational scholars to engage in a more fulsome outline of their philosophical tradition. A colleague with significant insights on the ontological basis of management education has commented to me that the Rational School rejects any discussion of ontology. To the extent that Rational scholarship represents a pragmatic endeavour which remains suspicious of empirical science, this comment is true. However, it remains that there is a significant body of work which underlies a rational pragmatic approach to knowledge. Rational scholars might find it helpful to rediscover pieces by Peirce (1878, 1901), James (1922), and Dewey (1929), and leverage these in reconsidering Pierson (1959), Gordon and Howell (1959), and Boyer (1990). There is also opportunity for Rational scholars to trace a line from these original pragmatic philosophies through to the practice-based scholarship of today (e.g. Jarzabkowski & Whittington, 2008a) and consider complementarities and contradictions between the two perspectives.

To engage in such research, Rational scholars may find opportunity in re-examining seminal works in the intellectual field such as Gordon and Howell (1959), Pierson (1959), and Boyer (1990) from a perspective of rational pragmatism. While Critical scholars might argue that such reports typify the Rational School (McLaren, 2019), there appears much about the critique of Rational scholarship as a scientific endeavour which seems to resemble a straw man fallacy, where the Rational position is misrepresented by the other schools and where critique is set up against this version (Johnson & Blair, 1983). Insights on the tradition of rational pragmatism would suggest that such a conclusion is conflated. Rational scholars might find re-examination of the original Ford and Carnegie reports a useful means for examining distinctions between pragmatism and scientific empiricism. Taken in this light, there is opportunity for Rational scholarship to arrive at different interpretations of the Carnegie and Ford reports.

If the pragmatism/empirical science relationship can be demonstrated to have been conflated, then one corollary of pushing back against such an interpretation by Critical scholars is that it would allow Rational scholars to investigate the extent to which management education has ever achieved the scientific threshold set out for it in the late 1950s. In the event it is established the field has not met such aspirations, Rational scholars should find fertile ground in considering implications of any such shortfall.

Questions on beliefs for scholars to consider in advancing the future of management education research:

- What are the complementarities and contradictions between approaches to knowledge based on rational pragmatism and scientific empiricism? To what extent can the two co-exist?
- Does the link between Rational management education and scientific empiricism represent a straw man argument?
- Does scholarship in management education resemble the field of scientific enquiry set out for it by Gordon and Howell (1959) and Pierson (1959)?

A second topic for exploration might be around radicalism in management education. It would seem the Critical School has benefited from portraying its scholarship as an outsider-driven, radical endeavour. A common Critical refrain is a rallying cry against the perceived profit-driven approaches to management education of the Rational School (e.g. McCann et al., 2020). However, one does not have far to look to suggest that the relativistic ethics and individual identity-driven agenda of the Critical School have been advantageous to the neoliberal enterprise.

As outlined in Chapter 4, the dominant Critical School has pushed a view of the neoliberal corporation (including the neoliberal business school) as an institution of oppression from which it believes individuals must be emancipated (Nordback et al., 2022). For Critical scholars, the modern capitalist institution creates gross economic and social outcomes (Fotaki & Prasad, 2015). It is racist (Edmondson et al., 2020), sexist (Mathieu, 2009), environmentally exploitative (Bergman et al., 2014), and western ethnocentric (Neal & Finlay, 2008). The response from the Critical School has been to push a progressive education which advances racial, sexual, and earthly emancipation from these repressive features of institutional neoliberalism.

Critical School scholars might reflect on evidence which suggests that not only do these neoliberal corporations appear to be enthusiastically adopting such concerns, but they are also furthering themselves in the process. Examples are numerous and cannot be adequately covered in a short space. However, the following appear to be illustrative. Where Critical issues on sexual identity, such as gay and transexual athletes, were once considered taboo topics, the weight of corporate money now supports players who 'come out'. Carl Nassib, the first openly gay player in America's NFL, was successful in sourcing over US$1 million in funding from Financial Finesse Ventures for developing a social media platform (Sprung, 2022), while his shirt was the top-selling merchandise item across the NFL in the days after the declaration of his sexuality (ESPN, 2021). Meanwhile, other gay sportspersons such as US soccer player Megan Rapinoe have secured sponsorship from Nike, Samsung, Victoria's Secret, and Visa, while UK diver Tom Daley receives endorsements from Adidas, Argos, and Etihad Airways. LGBTQA+ marketing guru, Bob Witeck says, 'sexual orientation is a differentiator that makes the brand popular with younger generations in ways they could never have imagined before. It suggests the company and the brand are welcoming, inclusive, and reflect the generation of today' (Moreau, 2021).

Transgender athletes are now also receiving corporate endorsement. Perhaps the world's best-known transgender athlete is 1970s American track and field star, Caitlyn Jenner. On transitioning to a woman in 2015, Jenner was paid US$5 million dollars by NBC Universal Television for producing an eight-part documentary series called *I Am Cait*, which focuses on her post-transition life and role as a transgender advocate (Allcot, 2021). Meanwhile, Adidas represents Layshia Clarendon, the WNBA's first openly transgender and non-binary player (*Sports Business Journal*, 2021), and US transgender duathlon representative Chris Mosier features on television ads for Nike (Nyad, 2016).

Corporations also appear to have embraced the racial interests promoted by Critical scholars. On the 2020 death of George Floyd at the hands of a white male police officer, there was a surge of corporate support for the Black Lives Matter movement. Firms such as Cisco, Etsy, IBM, Microsoft, Peloton, Uber, and PayPal not only contribute to Black Lives Matter, they also commit to other racial initiatives. Peleton has promised to invest US$100 million over four years to take on racial inequality, while Microsoft is investing US$150 million in its diversity and inclusion programme (Bass, 2020). As one of the world's largest corporations, Apple supports Black History Month and provides items such as a special-edition Apple Watch Black Unity Sport Loop, as well as a new matching watch face and iPhone wallpaper (Apple, 2023). Netflix uses Black History Month to present Black sitcom collections (Jabali,

2021). This snapshot of developments suggests that rather than being rejected by the corporation, Critical School identity-based movements are not only embraced, but they are monetised by it as well.

Similarly, for the criticism offered by Critical scholars of the neoliberal business school as a greedy and ethically bankrupt endeavour (e.g. Parker, 2018a), one might expect universities to show a reluctance to embrace such thinking. Indeed, this premise is at the heart of Critical scholarship on challenges of being a Critical early career academic, where the contention is made that such pursuits may be career limiting (Bristow et al., 2017). However, it is possible to point to many Critical scholars for whom their resistance does not appear to have had adverse career consequences. Martin Parker, as perhaps the most prominent critic of the business school, is a professor. Of the ten Critical Editors and Associate Editors at ML, seven are either professors or associate professors. Of the seven self-declared Critical scholars serving as Chief or Associate Editors on AMLE, five are either professors or associate professors.

In these circumstances, it would seem a worthwhile scholarly pursuit for academics to enquire on the radical nature of the Critical School. One path for exploring such an idea might come through the works of Italian philosopher, Augusto Del Noce. Arguing that progressive modernity is the only idea which remains out of the realm of critique by Critical scholars, Del Noce presents the contention that such scholarship is inherently conservative, and indeed has created 'the most conservative society that ever existed' (Del Noce & Lancellotti, 2017, p.44). Del Noce's view is that by its failure to conceive of a bad revolution, the Critical position becomes entirely a negation of all that has come before it and therefore rejects the possibility of renewal and reform which is intrinsic to tradition (Del Noce & Lancellotti, 2015). The work of Del Noce would therefore seem fertile ground for considering the radical nature of Critical scholarship.

A related project might focus on the nature of revolution itself. Calhoun's (1983) archaeology of revolutions suggests that traditional cultural values are essential to many radical movements. His analysis argues that this situation occurs because traditions provide populations with the internal social organisation necessary for radical collective action, and their goals are 'radically incompatible' with modern capitalist-dominated social formations (Calhoun, 1983, p.886). In these circumstances, scholars could consider whether it might be that a retreat to traditions as advocated by the Postliberal School represents a greater potential for revolution. Might the divine metaphysics of Postliberal faith represent a springboard for alternative perspectives? Songwriter Nick Cave perhaps hints at such a relationship, when he argues there is a 'spiritual audacity' in his return to the Christian Church and faith, 'a kind of reckless refusal to submit to the condition of the world' (Williams, 2023). In turn, a faith-based knowledge therefore offers '[a search for] something beyond which the rational world could offer us' (Cave & O'Hagan, 2022, pp.30–32). Scholars interested in this topic might therefore consider whether the resuscitation of Indigenous and ancient perspectives on knowledge and wisdom by the Critical School (e.g. Woods et al., 2022) offers a springboard for a radicalism set in tradition. Overall, it would seem that there is opportunity for scholars seeking to consider the nature of radicalism more formally in management education.

Questions on beliefs for scholars to consider in advancing the future of management education research:

- What is the relationship between Critical scholarship and the neoliberal corporation?
- What is the nature of radicalism in management education? How might it progress in the future?

Another topic which would seem ripe to consider is on the relationship between the management education teacher and authority. As has been discussed, the aim of the Critical School in management education is to seek student emancipation from all forms of authority. This emancipatory intent includes exposing oppressive power structures of the business school (Parker, 2018a), the textbook (Cameron et al., 2003), leading theories (Bridgman et al., 2019), and the curricula (Doucette et al., 2021). The emancipatory intent of Critical management educators is illustrated in topics related to power structures around issues of race (Ferraro, 2023) and sexual identity (Lo, 2023).

At the heart of such endeavours is a critical social imperative to emancipate the student. This imperative is one increasingly echoed in the management education literature, with Greenberg and Hibbert (2022, p.166) calling for educators to 'advocate for positive change' by moving away from a 'wilful ignorance' of the inequity of economic growth. However, it seems worthwhile to consider how this call for a more activist teaching model matches with an overall Critical intent to emancipate the other from all forms of authority.

Scholars seeking to investigate this seeming contradiction might consider power relations inherent in the shift from the sage on the stage to the guide on the side style of teaching characteristic of experiential learning. While early management education writing sought to grapple with underlying structures of authority in experiential learning (Akin, 1984), this theme appears to have lost currency in more contemporary literature. Yet, as Akin goes on to say, for the experiential educator to try and deny the authority inherent to their role so they won't be labelled authoritarians 'just seems to deny the nature of the situation in which we often find ourselves' (1984, pp.68–69). While such issues seem a likely fit for investigations on the shadow side of experiential learning (e.g. Taylor, 2018; Zidulka & Kajzer Mitchell, 2018), they are yet to feature in this literature. A revival of interest in investigating issues of authority on experiential learning might therefore fit with the emerging theme.

Underlying beliefs suited to exploring the link between the activist teacher and authority might be found in the Postliberal tradition, where the distinction between teachers and learners is a source of intellectual pursuit. C.S. Lewis explores this topic in his essay, *The Abolition of Man* (1975). Focusing on the relationship between man and nature, Lewis argues that each generation exercises power over its successors by modifying the environment they bequeath to future generations. Lewis contends that educators who decide on what is good and bad for humanity ultimately must define good and bad for others. In this process, Lewis presents a view that such teachers cannot be motivated by anything other than their own pleasure. Labelling people who seek to control nature as 'conditioners', Lewis illustrates how such control 'turns out to be a power exercised by some men [*sic*] over other men [*sic*] with Nature as its instrument' (Lewis, 1975, p.69).

Lewis argues that conditioners will initially perceive themselves as servants and guardians of humanity and conceive of themselves as acting in the good. As this process unfolds, Lewis contends that the conditioners must eventually reach the point where they decide what it is that others happen to like, from food and drink and sexual intercourse, through to even the length of life and preservation of the species. Eventually, every moral motive on which the conditioners might fall back in justifying their definition of the good for others becomes a logical fallacy. Lewis believes that the eventual position a conditioner must reach is one of '*sci volo, sic jeubeo*', thus I wish, thus I command (Lewis, 1975, p.77). The work of Lewis might therefore represent one opportunity for more formally considering issues of teacher authority in management education.

Questions on beliefs for scholars to consider in advancing the future of management education research:

*   What is the relationship between authority and the teacher in management education?

QUESTIONS ON PRACTICES IN THE FIELD OF MANAGEMENT EDUCATION

Turning attention to the terrain already covered in this book suggests several questions scholars may like to explore on underlying practices of the schools. It is suggested that there are grounds to investigate the empirical basis of the Rational School, engage in reflexive identity practice around the outsider role of the Critical management educator, and consider the traditional nature of scholarship in the Postliberal School.

For the tinkerer teacher in the Rational School, there appears the potential for seizing on trends at the macro level to pursue their scholarship. As an example, the Critical movement in the 1980s was motivated by taking a position against the economically rational policies of Reagan and Thatcher (Snell, 1986). The outcome of such a stance has seen Critical scholars able to leverage a burgeoning Critical ideology in publications such as *New Socialist* (e.g. Jacobs, 1988) and *New Left Review* (e.g. Mobasser, 1987) for introducing a range of new thinking to the management education literature. This treatment of management education as a 'big picture social science' (Lindebaum, 2023), where scholars leverage developments at the macro and micro levels to build a case for their scholarship, continues to drive Critical research agendas.

Similarly, there appears to be opportunity for Rational scholars to succeed in the practice side of their craft by seizing on macro trends to further their teaching and research pursuits. Rational scholars were successful in leveraging the Ford (Gordon & Howell, 1959) and Carnegie (Pierson, 1959) reports in developing an approach to management education intended for producing sound business graduates to feed into the American national project. However, while links between macro-level forces and the management education classroom appear in the adoption of pedagogies around topics such as environmental sustainability and diversity, equity, and inclusion, the Rational School seem to have been followers in such conversations.

Just as Critical scholars were able to seize on late 1980s Soviet developments in philosophy around *glasnost* and *perestroika* for driving a burgeoning development in their approach (Snell, 1989), it seems possible that Rational scholars could capture some of the intellectual energy of the emerging conservative movement in Europe for developing the aims and ambitions of their school. In a management education field which regularly presents its opposition to neoliberalism, might it also be that the *Wall Street Journal* and the *Economist* could one day represent for Rational scholars the equivalent of the *New Socialist*? Just as Rational scholars have the chance to better explain the roots of rational pragmatism as observed in Peirce and Dewey, so too might they grasp the potential in exploring sources of intellectual developments for shaping the nature of their management education approach?

One intriguing possibility for the Rational School and its view on positive aspects of authority might present through reinvigoration of the sage on the stage approach to teaching. Perhaps the archetype of the showrunner (Ryazanova et al., 2021) with its staged movie-style technological effects might offer new opportunities for rekindling this teaching format? Certainly, the enthusiasm of younger generations to consume social media suggests an opportunity for educators to seize chances to engage in content creation. Whatever the likely topics, it seems there is opportunity for Rational scholars to engage in more substantive debate around trends in the macro-environment and classroom pedagogies.

Questions on practices for scholars to consider in advancing the future of management education research:

- What is the relationship between micro-based action in Rational management education and the macro-environment of change in society?
- What are the possibilities of a sage on the stage approach to teaching in the digital age?

When it comes to Critical scholars, there seems opportunity to engage in reflexive identity practice on whether there is greater convergence between their scholarly work and what educational stakeholders demand in terms of classroom practice. As previously discussed, the fruits of Critical scholarship are now regularly monetised by corporations attuned to the segmentation possibilities offered by the rights-based and individual identity-driven agenda of the Critical School. Hence, Black History Month with its smartwatch faces and electronic device wallpapers (Apple, 2023). In a recent article, Hietanen and Mohammed (2023) acknowledge the ability of capitalist enterprises to 'readily co-opt even the most ardent criticism into its own ever-mutating paradigm'. Reflection by Critical scholars might engage with issues such as whether their position has emerged as the dominant scholarly paradigm in management education, and what this might mean for any personal identity based in being a rebellious outsider. If Critical scholars arrive at a similar view to Hietanen and Mohammed (2023) that their pedagogy contributes to the neoliberal engines of capital they seek to disintegrate, then it would suggest the need to explore reflexive identity questions related to being a Critical management educator.

Along these lines, perhaps there is the potential for a greater discussion of dissonance in management education? Studies show that individuals manage the dissonance created by a misfit in perceptions between actions and results by reconsidering their mental model of the world to either accommodate the difference, or act upon it in some way (Blackman et al., 2013). If research uncovers dissonance as a condition which afflicts Critical management educators, then there is the potential for work which considers how best to manage this challenge, and what it might mean for the future of Critical management education practice. To put forward one possible consideration, if Critical management education contributes to the success of the neoliberal corporation, then what techniques might the rebel teacher pursue for engaging in acts of corporate disruption?

Work which differentiates critique of emancipation from critique of improvement (Wallo et al., 2022) also appears to offer Critical scholars the opportunity to more formally consider the type of critique they practise in their classroom. Wallo et al. (2022) suggest three strategies for exploring different types of critique in a classroom setting. The first of these strategies occurs at the level of the business school, where courses dedicated to quality and production management are separated into a critique of improvement, while courses such as those on leadership and gender follow a critique for emancipation. The second strategy is to progress the two different forms of critique within a specific course by identifying appropriate topics for introducing a critique for improvement, and then associating other topics with a critique for emancipation. The authors' final suggestion is to synthesise both critiques within a course simultaneously, by training students in the ability to hold two opposing ideas in their minds at the same time.

In terms of the practice of being a Critical management educator, the continuum between different types of critique suggests a research programme around a rebel teacher's individual academic identity. There appears opportunity to more formally understand the different types of scholars who align with each individual school, and how differentiating themes might be evolving between scholarly types. For instance, will there emerge a more pronounced differentiation in the Critical School between Critical Pragmatists and Critical Radicals? And what might a philosophical continuum look like within the Critical School?

Further to this topic, Critical Radicals may need to consider how they can continue to progress the deconstruction of traditions which already appear to have been disintegrated. Here, the cycle we have witnessed in management education may prove instructive. In the best part of two decades, the more sharply critical end of Critical management education has progressed from the idea of textbooks as managerial propaganda (Mir, 2003), to a notion that the business school is American hegemony (Neal & Finlay, 2008), to an understanding of management education as a hidden curriculum of tooth-and-claw capitalism (Parker, 2018a), and finally to a view that management education is white supremacy (Liu, 2022). Given the nature of this trajectory, it seems worthwhile to consider what future attempts at deconstruction of western traditions might look like, and how they might fit into a management education classroom.

Questions on practices for scholars to consider in advancing the future of management education research:

- What is the relationship between the practice of Critical management teaching and the neoliberal corporation?
- Is dissonance evidenced in the academic identity of Critical management educators?

- How is the concept of critique practised in the Critical management education classroom?
- What might comprise a philosophical continuum of critique in Critical management education? What are the likely implications of such a continuum for classroom and scholarly practice?
- How might deconstruction progress on western traditions which already appear disintegrated?

A scholarly programme considering the career and academic identity of the foolish educator of the Postliberal School might find opportunity in exploring existential challenges of preserving individual identity in circumstances where scholarly publishing is difficult and preferred classical pedagogical techniques do not meet immediate corporate skills-based needs. Reflecting on some of the work which might be considered Postliberal over the past decade, it appears that the craft of such scholarship and practice is being performed at institutions away from the top tier. This suggests the possibility of exploring whether there might be pockets of institutions which might be more immune to the performative targets of the university (Jones et al., 2020), where different types of scholarship could thrive.

Questions on practices for scholars to consider in advancing the future of management education research:

- What contexts and circumstances might promote outlier types of management education research?

The above practice-based research agendas suggest there is potential in exploring how different worlds of the relevant schools are brought into the classroom. In undertaking this book, I have been struck by the serendipitous way my own strategic management course has come to comprise elements of all three schools. The first phase of the course is of a Rational School basis, where students are taught to apply various frameworks such as PESTEL (Aguilar, 1967) and Five Forces analysis (Porter, 1979). The second phase of the course is more Critical, where students are introduced to topics on the power, politics, and storytelling of strategy implementation (Barry & Elmes, 1997; Clegg et al., 2023). The final phase of the course is Postliberal, where students reflect on their own strengths and weaknesses for developing a deeper understanding of how they might navigate future career challenges.

One research topic which therefore might be worth contemplating is how educators evidence the schools in their management education classroom. Do they tend to pursue one type of approach? Or are multiple approaches in evidence? If there is a suggestion that many management educators adopt elements of the different schools, then it might be worthwhile considering the promise which lies in the theoretical concept of diagonalisation. Coming from a Biblical Studies philosophy that the world too often splits issues into false cultural dichotomies, diagonalisation presents a both/and approach to understanding biblical messages. For example, Christ in the Bible is both God and human, as well as leader and servant. Diagonalisation is an opportunity to overcome the trend of opposites where people 'define themselves as the negative image of their enemy', and instead offers a 'radical intervention … challenging us to reconsider our assumptions, leaving the initial dichotomized options appearing bland and unappealing by comparison' (Watkin & Keller, 2022, pp.19–20). In terms of applying diagonalisation to an academic career in management education, it is worthwhile considering whether we might be able to take the best of the three schools in our teaching practice. Might it be that there are ways of developing our academic identity in a way which enables us to simultaneously identify with more than one school?

Questions on practices for scholars to consider in advancing the future of management education research:

- How do management educators evidence the three schools of management education in their classroom practice?
- How might management educators diagonalise their academic identity to identify with different approaches to management education?

Skills-based educational practice appears to face challenges related to how to keep up with the needs of the corporation, and how to provide effective training. Trends come and go. A history of the field presents a graveyard of disused and superseded curricula. Perhaps the best example comes regarding technology, where accelerated innovation cycles bring new developments in shorter and shorter time periods (Marshall, 2018). Casting our eyes over the archives of management education scholarship unearths topics devoted to building student skills in using microcomputers (Bigelow, 1986), undertaking modelling and scenario analysis (Wheelwright, 1972; DuBrin, 1992), and adopting interactive television (Hall, 1996). Such advances have either subsequently ceded into an ongoing technological revolution or have become so ubiquitous as to be unremarkable. It is not unreasonable to suggest that current trends in data analytics (Calvard, 2016), or around specific forms of social media (Middleton, 2022), are likely to head the same way.

Keeping up with such trends is not only challenging for the educator in terms of adopting pedagogical innovations which might become obsolete, there are also potential career implications. In reflecting on the late 1990s rise of the internet, Bilimoria (1999) outlines the downside for the management educator of the time and energy required for harnessing the teaching applications of the then-emerging information technologies. As Harley (2019) opines, it is not always the case that the energies required to ensure outstanding teaching are viewed favourably by universities. Fitting such pedagogical innovation into an ongoing academic career can therefore provide a challenge.

A perhaps deeper concern for the skills-based approach to the Rational School is whether the tinkerer approach of providing students with workplace skills is one which works. It is often said that business leaders face an increasingly complex and interdependent world (Colby et al., 2011). One finding across many employer surveys is that these same leaders hold conflicted views on the quality of graduates entering their workforce (Bauer-Wolf, 2018). A continuing area of concern for Rational scholars is that their efforts to bring ethics into management education seem to have largely failed to translate to changes in organisational behaviour (Simha et al, 2012). For example, a study by Dean and Beggs (2006) finds that business school faculty believe they have little or no impact on a student's ethical behaviours.

Such evidence suggests the challenge of implementing an effective Rational School approach to scholarship. From the perspective of implementing a skills-based pedagogy, the tinkerer educator appears to have a relatively straightforward path open to such innovation by pursuing the industry linkages of which universities are encouraging. Yet, without the more critical perspectives inherent to the Critical and Postliberal schools, it is difficult to see how the Rational School can offer more than a reactive response to corporate demand. Similar to issues on the type of critique leveraged by Critical scholars in their classroom, Rational scholars might also find fertile ground in more deeply contemplating the concept of a critique for improvement. A type of critical reflection employed to improve current practices (Wallo et al., 2022), the position would seem consistent with the approach to knowledge inherent to a tradition built on rational pragmatism (Peirce, 1878). Interested scholars might leverage insights on improvement for considering issues related to skills-based training in management education.

Questions on practices for scholars to consider in advancing the future of management education research:

- How can skills-based management education stay ahead of the needs of the corporation?

A second practice-based concern relates to the role of technology in management education. Over time, management education appears to have offered only limited critique on technology and its use in organisations. Boddy and Buchanan (1984) note job losses and the emergence of new types of jobs as possible consequences of a rise in information technology. More recently, concerns have emerged over the marginalisation of women and ethnic minorities in tech-driven occupations (Parsley, 2022), as well as the instability and uncertainty of work in the gig economy (Caza, 2020). But, largely, the role of technology in organisations and management education remains unexplored.

Reflecting on the emergence of the issue of power in management education might prove instructive. The topic was originally surfaced through book reviews (e.g. Whitley, 1977), before becoming a mainstream concern (e.g. Tosey, 1989). In this vein, it is worth noting the work of Endrissat (2021) in reviewing Jennifer Rhee's (2018) book *The Robotic Imaginary*. In this work, Rhee exposes the exclusion and dehumanisation of transhumanists in using automated and predictive technologies to manage, control, and surveille the human workforce (Endrissat, 2021).

A similar Critical line of thinking is reflected in the apparent main critique on technology in management education provided by Moser and colleagues (2022) in their take on the impacts of artificial intelligence (AI) algorithms on human morality. In this piece, the authors express concern that morality which relies on judgement will irrevocably change through AI systems because they possess agency which informs, guides, and steers human judgement. Concluding that AI tools are not innocent tools in decision making, the authors argue for (in)action in encouraging management educators to question taken-for-granted assumptions of decision making informed by AI. Perhaps this work and the rapid rise of AI technologies might see management education scholars take a new interest in the topic.

Authors seeking to make a contribution in this area are likely to find opportunity in the realm of wider sociological thought, where damaging effects of technology are explored from perspectives of sexism and individual rights. For example, journalist Nancy Jo Sales (2016) explores social media from a critical feminist perspective in her book *American Girls: Social Media and the Secret Lives of Teenagers*. Sales sets out what she argues are sexist undertones on a range of technological trends. While allegations persist that Kris Jenner, mother of celebrity megastar Kim Kardashian, deliberately leaked the sex tape which made her daughter famous, less well known is the story of Taylen Cald. Two-year-old Cald had 112,000 followers on Instagram and her mother was impressed that her daughter had become a brand. However, Taylen's mother also subsequently reported that she was concerned her daughter's images were being copied and shared on other Instagram pages, some of which were 'of a sexually pornographic nature' (Sales, 2016, p.33).

Sales' interest in a feminist presentation of the challenges with social media appear partially motivated by an earlier piece, *What Silicon Valley Thinks of Women* (Burleigh, 2015). Exploring what she describes as a 'savagely misogynistic' culture, Burleigh details Silicon Valley and a range of sexual misdemeanours ranging from sexual jokes to gender-based hiring and firing, and sexual harassment lawsuits. The article features the 2013 case of Gurbaksh Chahal, dubbed one of Silicon Valley's most eligible bachelors, whose home video security camera captured him physically assaulting his girlfriend for half an hour. Chahal subsequently received 25 hours of community service. In a later case, in 2016 Chahal was found to have committed acts of domestic violence against a woman and served six months in prison. Yet, Chahal's net worth is now believed to have more than doubled from the 2011 estimate of US$150 million (Sine, 2011), and he has gone on to found other companies as well as marry a Bollywood actress.

Even the most prominent Silicon Valley names have been associated with questionable treatment of women. Prior to founding Facebook, in 2003 Mark Zuckerberg launched a site called FaceMash. Derived from the then-popular HOTorNOT website, FaceMash hacked into university web servers to download photos of students without their permission, and then placed photos of female students next to each other so that fellow students could vote on their attractiveness (Horton, 2018). Meanwhile, internal investigations at Microsoft and the Bill and Melinda Gates Foundation suggest that Microsoft founder Bill Gates actively pursued women in both organisations while married. Farrell (2021) says that while Gates is portrayed as a 'lovable "dad" tech tycoon … he's an unfaithful predatory guy … there's no equality when it comes to a man like him'.

Management education scholars seeking to critique technology might find Zuboff's (2019) *The Age of Surveillance Capitalism* on the convergence of knowledge, authority, and power to be of interest. The book represents the culmination of a series of works where Zuboff traces the emergence in the early 2000s at Google of the monetisation of a new type of capital which harnesses data in a predictive capacity for modifying human behaviour to create commercial opportunities (Zuboff et al., 2019). Zuboff argues that surveillance capitalism is an endeavour which claims human experience as free raw material, creates an unprecedented concentration of wealth, knowledge, and power, provides a framework for surveillance, and represents a coup from above which overthrows people's sovereignty (Zuboff, 2019).

Providing an archaeology of surveillance capitalism, Zuboff notes its origins in the work of Google's Chief Economist, Hal Varian. Varian identifies four uses of the computer in everyday transactions, including data extraction and analysis, new contractual forms due to better monitoring, personalisation and customisation, and continuous experiments (Varian, 2010). Varian's thoughts play out at Google through machine intelligence, algorithmic production, and predictive analysis. These capabilities enable the firm to develop targeted advertising and build wealth rapidly, but the mindset also enables Google to harvest data in new ways. For example, when a web search is undertaken Google collects a range of collateral data, such as the number and pattern of search terms, how a query is phrased, dwell times, click patterns, and location (Zuboff, 2019).

Scholars interested in exploring the topic of technology in management education might also find opportunity in considering a Postliberal position. In his essay on why he doesn't use a computer, Berry (2000) articulates technological progression as a process which discards not only the former technology, but also people involved in its production and subsequent use. In this light, technology is therefore antithetical to a common humanity. C.S. Lewis also provides a critique of technology as having an adverse impact on future generations. While noting that humans revel in the technologies and science they have created and the apparent power over nature these advancements provide, Lewis argues that these same technologies and sciences weaken subsequent generations because 'we have pre-ordained how they are to use them' (Lewis, 1975, p.70). In describing technology as the enabler of a totalising conservative society, Del Noce argues that it destroys any revolutionary impulse by creating a superficial impression of a liberating explosion while, in essence, reducing it to a consumer good (Del Noce & Lancellotti, 2015). To provide one example, Postliberals would likely consider the development of electric cars as about consumerism rather than environmentalism. Taken together, the Critical sociological and Postliberal perspectives suggest opportunity for scholars to take renewed interest in exploring the nexus between technology and management education.

Questions on practices for scholars to consider in advancing the future of management education research:

•   What is the role of technology in management education?

Existential questions abound for Postliberal School scholars. One immediate observation is that this is a school which is fledgling. While JME carries scholarship with a Postliberal flavour from authors such as Jerry Harvey, Peter Vaill, and Gib Aiken, the high-water mark for Postliberal management education seems to have arrived nearly three decades ago with Peter Vaill's (1996) *Learning as a Way of Being*. Other than a few pieces on setting up classroom exercises for assisting students to develop their character through an understanding of virtue (e.g. Eriksen et al., 2019), there is little currently in management education to suggest a rush towards contemporary scholarship which explores Postliberal themes.

A prime challenge for Postliberals is how to engage with a world which is characterised by the globalism and technology they set themselves against. It seems a noble concern to support local communities and families by acts such as purchasing groceries at the mum and dad corner stores which existed in the 1950s and 1960s, but these stores have long been replaced by major supermarket chains and warehouse operations. Similarly, while Wendell Berry might continue to work on pen and paper without a computer (Kingsnorth, 2018), the Postliberal management educator is confronted by a range of technological systems to which their employers have entered commercial obligations at great expense and with an expectation of implementation. Even were Postliberal educators to follow prescriptions suggested by Christian metaphysical traditions for preserving their religion in the face of progress, such as returning to Benedictine community living (Dreher, 2019), such suggestions would seem incompatible with the globalised commercial university.

Important to any Postliberal scholars seeking a revival of their school will be how they might develop a community from which proponents can thrive. Given that any Postliberal movement would currently appear fledgling, it is also likely that such a community would need to develop in a manner which accounts for geographic distance. While virtual learning communities have long featured in the management education literature (Allan, 2007), impetus provided by the COVID-19 pandemic may serve to guide Postliberals in how to build the links necessary for sustaining their school. However, contradictions between such an approach and cautious Postliberal views on technology are apparent.

Ironically, work performed by Critical scholars in terms of building community between marginalised communities (Dodd et al., 2022) may be helpful to Postliberals in terms of determining how a sustainable cohort can be developed. Where such efforts have focused on people with disabilities and how to build their confidence and social capital, it is worthwhile for Postliberals as a minority group to consider how the learning from these programmes, and how they engage in practices such as mentoring and financial support to create a thriving community, could be leveraged across other domains. Whatever the approach, it would seem important for Postliberal scholars to consider how they might pursue community within their school.

Questions on practices for scholars to consider in advancing the future of management education research:

- Given the pervasive nature of technology and capitalism in the modern university, is it possible to be Postliberal in management education?
- How might the Postliberal School build a thriving community in the current management education environment?

QUESTIONS ON INSTITUTIONS IN THE FIELD OF MANAGEMENT EDUCATION

If we are to consider institutions in the intellectual field of management education as comprising the leading journals, then the preceding work also identifies several questions which scholars may like to investigate. It is suggested that there are grounds to consider differentiation between the three journals, how to encourage original scholarship, the role of special issues in management education, and the potential for other forms of publishing. As has been noted in research opportunities around the nature of radicalism in management education, Editors and Associate Editors at the leading journals now represent mainly Critical scholars. Recent publications across AMLE, ML, and JME also appear to capture a Critical intent. Titles with a Critical focus are seemingly commonplace. Recent publications include: 'Disrupting Privilege as Power and Control: Re-imagining business and the appreciation of Indigenous stewardship in management education curricula' (Young-Ferris & Voola, 2023), 'How We Learn Whiteness: Disciplining and resisting management knowledge' (Liu, 2022), and 'Impact and University Business Training Courses Delivered to the Marginalized: A systematic review' (Dodd et al., 2022). There would seem to be an opportunity for scholars to consider implications of this Critical turn for the institutional field of publishing in management education.

One question which could be asked is whether the management education field can sustain three journals of a broadly Critical nature. The publishing arena is a highly competitive one, and it may be that it is worth considering the degree of differentiation between the journals and whether these are sufficient to allow all three of them to survive?

Scholars might like to undertake more formal bibliometric analyses to determine levels of differentiation between the journals. Are published materials indeed converging on a Critical perspective? Or does there remain a broader scholarship represented within the body of works? One launchpad for undertaking such analysis might be the context provided by the post-COVID-19 period. Just as COVID-19 provided an opportunity to focus on business schools' practices of value proposition, creation, exchange, and capture (Laasch et al., 2022a), the opportunity seems ripe for exploring similar topics in management education publishing. In an anecdotal sense, my own involvement with two of these journals means I am aware that the post-COVID-19 period has seen a significant drop in the number of manuscript submissions. Conference attendees at workshops involving management education journals are likely to be informed that desk rejection rates remain high, with many submitted manuscripts apparently poorly targeted and out of scope. In such circumstances, it would seem there might be the chance for management education scholars to use content analyses and other qualitative methods for considering what has been published and determining whether the post-2022 content is reflective of that which has gone before it. If notable changes can be determined, then a useful project would be to explore whether there are greater fundamentals at play.

If analysis discerns a greater convergence to Critical scholarship, then other promising research agendas might present. A greater convergence could lead to interesting topics around issues such as journal sustainability. For a long period of time, the field appears to have been well differentiated. ML represented Critical scholarship, JME represented Rational scholarship and contained an earlier undercurrent of Postliberal scholarship, while AMLE was a mix of Critical and Rational voices.

However, participants at paper development workshops are now likely to hear that the two matters on which AMLE would most like to differentiate itself are related to the business of business schools (McLaren et al., 2021) and big picture societal impacts of management education (Lindebaum, 2023). These topics are both Critical endeavours, suggesting that differentiation might be becoming less about contrasting philosophies, and more about different types of Critical critique. Perhaps it is noteworthy that ML, the most Critical of the management education journals, has provided a recent article which would appear more at home with a Postliberal perspective. Called 'Phronetic Improvisation: A virtue ethics perspective' (Hadjimichael & Tsoukas, 2023), this development might provide some indication of the challenges of differentiation within the field.

Furthermore, different types of manuscripts are also likely to follow a Critical intent. AMLE's advice to scholars on producing publishable essays which offer 'disciplined provocation' (Hibbert, 2018) is built on the call from well-known Critical scholar Hugh Willmott for 'provocations to a debate' found in his early Critical management education paper (1994). In considering the four key characteristics of an AMLE essay, it is worth noting the final requirement displays Critical intent by issuing 'a call for action' (Hibbert, 2018). This advice suggests essays are likely to be Critical in nature.

If theoretical differentiation between the journals is indeed fading, it is worthwhile asking what such a development might mean for the future of the journals. With the *British Journal of Management* (A ranking) now also entering the field of management education, it would seem the time is ripe for asking such questions.

Questions on institutions for scholars to consider in advancing the future of management education research:

- What is the level of differentiation between journals in the field of management education?
- How does management education research published in the post-COVID-19 period compare with that which came prior to the pandemic?

If there is Critical convergence, scholars could consider what this development might mean for the sourcing of quality manuscripts. It is noteworthy that the April 2023 edition of JME features only three articles, one of which is a holdover from the special issue on privilege. Does this situation on the volume of quality manuscripts represent an outlier? Or is it potentially a pointer to an underlying greater dynamic?

The journals appear to be making significant efforts to solicit quality manuscripts. Paper development workshops are common, and presentations at major conferences on how to publish in the journals represent a regular feature of the academic calendar. Editors in the field have consistently provided guidance to would-be authors on expected standards around published works. Research pieces are rejected on lack of originality, non-meaningful implications for theory and/or practice, and poor empirical methods (Edwards & Leigh, 2022). Essays are rejected for providing insufficient grounds for disciplined provocation (Hibbert, 2018).

However, while guidance is often provided on making empirical contributions (Hamdani et al., 2023), there seems to have been less direction given on issues of originality. One reasonable launchpad for encouraging original contributions might be in further explicating the worlds of the three schools, particularly in terms of their approaches to knowledge and ethics. As Laasch and colleagues (2022a) observe, journal articles in management education publications rarely disclose an author's underlying philosophical position. In terms of prompting greater originality in published manuscripts, a useful project would be to continue beyond what has been presented in this book in terms of providing greater detail on the foundational beliefs inherent to the different worlds of management education. Such a step promises to provoke scholars towards greater reflection on their own underlying beliefs and better understand where they might contribute to original scholarship in the intellectual field.

It is also worth considering whether publishing requirements serve to limit originality in the field. Harvey's (1979) Postliberal piece 'Learning To Not Teach' has been recognised with a Lasting Impact Award by JME. In that the article offers advice such as 'I don't take responsibility for what others learn', Harvey (1979, p.19) appears to meet the hurdle for providing original thought and provocation. However, Harvey's piece does not conform to current conventions around scholarly practice. It presents a series of opinions with no confirmatory evidence. It is notable that in discussions around the Lasting Impact Award, one member of JME's associate editorial team put forward: 'as good as the thoughts he [Harvey] shares in the paper are, would it get published today?' (Middleton & Alday, 2023). It is difficult to conclude that such a piece would be publishable in the present institutional context. It is therefore worth considering how many potentially important provocations the field might miss out through the constraint of scholarly publishing conventions.

Questions on institutions for scholars to consider in advancing the future of management education research:

- How might we encourage originality of scholarship in management education?
- How might the intellectual field overcome the constraint of scholarly publishing conventions to encourage work which provokes conversations and moves them forward?

Perhaps on the back of the difficulty of sourcing quality manuscripts, one notable trend in the three leading management education journals is a rush to special issues. Recent or prospective special issues include features on learning through paradox (AMLE), unlearning (ML), mental health and well-being (JME), experiential learning in large classes (JME), doing careers differently (ML), new histories of business schools (AMLE), responsible management (ML), learning during COVID-19 (ML), the senses in management education (ML), positive perspectives in management learning (ML), privilege in business schools (JME), and the Fourth Industrial Revolution (4IR) (JME). These special issues have been published from 2020 or are to be published by 2024. The list does not include 50th anniversary special issues of ML published in 2020, or to be published in JME in 2025. It is worth considering whether the proliferation of special issues is a portrait of a healthy and thriving field, or whether it is a symptom of a scholarly malaise? Furthermore, is this development suggestive of a trend towards more niche areas of exploration?

Importantly, the field of management education is yet to debate the merits of special issues. However, management education scholars looking to investigate this issue might note a similar conversation held in the wider field of organisation studies. Investigating the matter of special issues, Priem (2006) analysed a sample of 33 combined publishing years for *Academy of Management Journal, Academy of Management Review*, and *Organization Studies*. His findings in a 15-year sample period were that special issue pages comprised more than 30 per cent of the total published pages. Priem's argument is that this high number of special issues squeezes out quality articles on other topics, and redirects scholars away from areas in which they may have already been researching and towards the focus of special issues. The latter issue is important, because Priem argues that innovative and creative scholarship is most likely to be generated by individual scholars pursuing their own scholarship. In a follow-up piece defending special issues, Mowday (2006) argues for journals to pursue broader topics when defining their special issues and for issues that aim to rekindle interest in topics that may have fallen off the agenda. Whatever the outcome, it would seem there is an opportunity for management education scholars to engage in similar debates over the proliferation of special issues in the field.

Questions on institutions for scholars to consider in advancing the future of management education research:

• What is special about special issues in management education?

A related question for Postliberal scholars seeking any revival of their school is around the paradox inherent to publishing material which seeks to progress knowledge by reviving classical traditions. The dearth of Postliberal articles published in management education journals since the turn of the twenty-first century is perhaps a pointer to the publishing challenges faced by scholars in this school.

The problem is one which appears to have been recognised by Postliberals. In his polemic on the difference between the notions of teaching and learning, Harvey (1979) argues for a new journal which focuses on learning over teaching. He contends, 'In my discipline, there is a journal called *Exchange: The Organizational Behavior Teaching Journal*. What if it were called *Exchange: The Organizational Behavior Learning Journal*? I'll bet the content of the articles would be very different and a lot more interesting' (1979, p.19). Such a journal would appear more consistent with Postliberal ideals, and perhaps create a more ready path for such scholarship.

Otherwise, Postliberals will need to test claims of existing publications that they are committed to a 'Big Table' approach to management education in which diverse theories are welcome (Foster, 2020). Yet, the progressive nature of management education in the Rational and Critical schools requires extension of knowledge in order to be published (Edwards & Leigh, 2022). There is inherent difficulty for Postliberals providing commentary based on timeless understandings to meet this standard. Greek and Roman classics may be eternal, but their centuries-old basis means they are hardly vehicles for progressing knowledge. Similarly, Postliberals are likely to find that the metaphysical nature of their approach to knowledge does not easily lend itself to theorising. As biblical scholar Fleming Rutledge argues, the Bible does not present theories. Instead, it contains stories, images, metaphors, symbols, sagas, sermons, songs, letters, and poems. 'It would be hard to find writing that is less theoretical' (Rutledge, 2015, p.29).

Modern day Postliberals may find it instructive that Jerry Harvey and Peter Vaill, the two most identifiable management education scholars writing within the school, published the majority of their works in essay form and in books and book chapters. In reflecting on the collection of Vaill's full body of lifetime work, Dent suggests that his mentor's view of himself as an essayist was 'much to the chagrin of his colleagues who were aghast that his work never included a structural equation model, multivariate analysis, or even a p-test' (2022, p.31). Even a cursory glance at 'Learning To Not Teach' (Harvey, 1979) and 'Exploration and Discovery' (Vaill, 1981) will likely lead to the conclusion that such pieces would never be published in the management education journals of today. These articles are provocative and exploratory, but they have very little of what would resemble the disciplined provocation required for publishing essays today (Hibbert, 2018).

Postliberals might therefore be primed to explore the wider publishing field in management education, such as books, podcasts, and other non-traditional forms of output. Indeed, Postliberals may be in a near unique position to test the boundaries of new types of publishing in the discipline and inform the wider intellectual field on emerging horizons.

Questions on institutions for scholars to consider in advancing the future of management education research:

• What media and outlets might represent the wider field of future publishing in management education?

QUESTIONS ON SOCIAL RELATIONS IN THE FIELD OF MANAGEMENT EDUCATION

The post-Enron period in management education appears notable for two developments. First, publication in management education journals now appears to require a commitment to at least a small-c critical improvement. Leading journals no longer publish pieces which do not explicitly move conversations forward.

This development has implications for publishing skills-based Rational educational innovations. Where teaching innovations were once the domain of JME and AMLE (e.g. Moore et al., 1992), such pieces are unlikely to contribute to theory or a critique for improvement (Wallo et al., 2022). In response, the Management and Organizational Behavior Teaching Society (MOBTS) has created a sister journal to JME, *Management Teaching Review* (MTR). MTR seeks to return to the field some of the immediately practical classroom techniques and practices which had featured in JME prior to its focus on Scholarship of Teaching and Learning (Forray & Dean, 2016). Consistent with this endeavour, the journal has published an array of useful pedagogical techniques which might have found a home in JME in the 1970s and 1980s, such as using films to teach about perception and decision-making biases (Rabinowitz & Fender, 2018), introducing exercises to improve students' capabilities in financial analysis (Carter, 2023), and using improvisation techniques to improve emotional intelligence (Shivarajan & Andrews, 2021).

The second development is suggested in the post-Millennium rise in articles with a more explicit Large-C Critical emancipatory intent. The first edition of ML in the year 2000 contains features on ideological invasion (Case & Selvester, 2000) and feminist portrayals of human resource development (Hughes, 2000). Such articles appear representative of a niche Critical scholarship in the field at the time, as contrasted with the corresponding edition of JME which examines governance challenges of graduate programmes (Dent, 2000) and decision models (Hamilton et al., 2000).

Once again, a more formal bibliometric analysis of trends and themes in the intellectual field would be useful in confirming the extent of this move, but all three of the major management education journals feature articles with an explicitly Large-C Critical intent. The development appears to have been accelerated by the 2020 death of George Floyd at the hands of Minneapolis police officers, a societal event which appears to have focused management educators on their own role in perpetuating hidden racist power structures. Where JME might once have represented the bastion of Rational scholarship, its response to the Floyd incident was to publish a special issue on privilege which focused on emancipatory topics relating to social class (Moergen & Kish-Gephart, 2023), activism (Ferraro, 2023), and intersectionality (Lo, 2023).

For a school which so long appeared to dominate the field of management education, it seems worthwhile asking whether the status of the Rational School is now eclipsed in the premier journals by the Critical School. Scholars contemplating the status of social relations in the intellectual field might consider whether there have been shifts in the editorial board make-up of the leading journals over time.

If a trend towards Critical scholarship is confirmed, then it is likely there are also important career implications. To this stage, the Critical School seems the only one in the management education field which appears to have undertaken a concerted attempt to identify risks of early career research in Scholarship of Teaching and Learning (Bristow et al., 2019; Ratle et al., 2020). However, it would appear worthwhile for scholars in other schools to engage in similar types of conversation.

Scholars of a Rational persuasion might consider the career implications associated with publishing. They could ask whether the teaching innovations which have sustained Rational School scholarship in the past, are now most likely to find a home in MTR. However, MTR faces systemic challenges which mean it is unlikely to sustain a typical teaching and research career. On the 2023 journal rating list from the Australian Business Dean's Council (ABDC), MTR has been added as a C-ranked journal. This is the lowest level for a ranked journal. While MTR pieces are likely to be impactful in terms of teachers in other geographies and universities taking up the published innovations, evidence to date suggests that scholars in other publications are unlikely to cite such pieces. As an example, papers published in the journal's inaugural issue on teaching teamwork (Hannah & Robertson, 2016), and using qualitative interviews in the classroom (Reardon, 2016), have received only six subsequent citations between them, and none of these comes from AMLE, ML, or JME.

Therefore, there appears to be opportunity for academics contemplating career implications for publishing Rational scholarship to consider the topic of citation metrics around the publication of teaching innovations. In particular, it would seem useful to consider where or how these might be improved. Similarly, it might be instructive to consider what type of career is most likely to be sustained through publishing on teaching innovations. Does such a path fit more naturally with teaching-focused academics, where the liminal nature of the career (Bamber et al., 2017) might provide a way to the third road of great teaching and research (Fukami, 2007)?

One outcome of a more Critical management education scholarship is that publication of Rational pieces is likely to be at a premium. In such circumstances, it will be important for editors to reaffirm their commitment to the 'Big Table' approach advocated at AMLE for theory-driven work from a variety of perspectives (Foster, 2020). Might there be a requirement for new sections in the leading journals, once again focused on disseminating classroom innovations? Rational scholars might do well to consider whether the implications of such publication are also likely to be in greater competition with other Rational scholars seeking an increasingly limited journal space. If it is shown that successful Rational scholars will have to display outstanding research skills to be published, then one research project might be around the skills base of Rational scholars and how these can be uplifted.

To make the grade, Rational scholars pursuing this traditional path are likely to need to demonstrate capability in reflecting an agenda in advance of business. Again, Rational scholars might investigate whether a critique for improvement (Wallo et al., 2022) offers a sustainable path to the leading journals. One template might be emerging in the more critical air which seems characteristic of Rational School thinking on the 4IR. While Fukami et al. (2022) take 4IR as an opportunity for using technologies to empower and engage employees, they also note the potential for these advances to sever relationships between workers and employers almost entirely. The capability to balance the pros and cons of corporate advances would appear necessary for the Rational School in pursuing scholarship in traditional outlets.

In a related vein, there would also seem to be an interesting project for Rational scholars to consider the career trajectories of their profession. If there becomes a more limited range of publishing opportunities for Rational scholars in traditional outlets, then might they retreat to administrator university careers? While questions have been raised on the compatibility between university administrative values and academic careers (Dean, 2018), university administrative work based on efficiency, market reach, and commercialisation appears consistent with the skills tinkerer teachers aim to foster in their students. Combining the busyness of administrative positions with research and teaching can often be a challenging task. However, Rational scholars investigating different career trajectories might consider the possibilities of scholarship which investigates administrator career trajectories. The nascent management education literature in the area of university administration (e.g. Stark, 2019), combined with the scale of business in many contemporary universities, suggests such a publishing path may be a worthwhile pursuit for Rational scholars.

Taken together, questions around the future of Rational scholarship in management education suggest an opportunity for scholars in this tradition to engage more deeply in topics related to the future of their school.

Questions on social relations for scholars to consider in advancing the future of management education research:

- What are the pitfalls and opportunities of scholarly careers in skills-based management education?
- What are the skills necessary for success in skills-based management education?
- How might a critique for improvement (Wallo et al., 2022) feed into a publishing career in management education?
- What are the possibilities of scholarship in business school administration for furthering careers in management education?

There appears an opportunity for Postliberal scholars to explore topics related to tradition and management education. Such a project is set against the success enjoyed by the Critical School in undermining traditional sources of authority for the Rational School including the university and business school (Parker, 2018a), and pedagogical tools such as the textbook (Mir, 2003). It also goes against initiatives by the Critical School to find a voice for other cultures in reviving Indigenous pedagogies. However, it does enable Postliberals to make different contributions to those which currently appear ascendant.

To investigate possibilities related to topics in tradition and management education, Postliberals might find inspiration in the works of Augusto Del Noce. The Italian philosopher argues that at the heart of the shift to a secular modern society is a radical atheism which offers itself as a complete break from the past. Del Noce's view is that proponents of the liberal society put forward the idea that modernity is the start of history. Modern philosophy asserts an axiological meaning that it represents 'a point of no return', and that 'today it is no longer possible' (Del Noce & Lancellotti, 2015, p.3). Del Noce asserts that while such a position provides a response to the totalitarian forces which emerged in World War II and enables the liberal society to position itself as anti-totalitarian, it also rejects traditions inherent to Fascistic resistance, such as Christianity and humanitarian socialism.

According to this perspective, liberalism rejects all forms of tradition including a supernatural and metaphysical understanding of religious transcendence, and a rejection of the possibility of God. According to Del Noce, the outcome of this line of thinking is a total libertine revolution which portrays any competing philosophy as reactionary. Society therefore disintegrates all notions of tradition, presenting it as antithetical to freedom and dismissing any possibility of a positive understanding of authority. Yet, as has been noted in the questions on beliefs in the intellectual field, Calhoun (1983) identifies successful revolutions as historically having been founded in artisans with some prosperity and privileges to defend who can mobilise communal bonds to draw on traditional cultural values. While there has been a small amount of investigative work on the possibilities of tradition in management education (e.g. Hibbert et al., 2018), there seems the possibility of expanding this line of enquiry. Postliberal scholars might therefore find opportunity in leveraging insights from Del Noce on tradition with Calhoun's understanding on the nature of revolutions, to investigate the possibilities of tradition for advancing management education.

Questions on social relations for scholars to consider in advancing the future of management education research:

• What are the promises and pitfalls of tradition in management education?

CONCLUSION

During the process of writing this book, there have been a number of global developments. Russia has invaded Ukraine, and has again brought war to Europe's door. COVID-19 continues to take lives, but the world has opened and travel now continues as though little ever happened. Colleagues occasionally nod at each other and smile about the lost years of 2020 and 2021. The launch of ChatGPT has seen numerous discussions on the rise of AI, not least from educators who seem concerned at its possible impact on student cheating. Inflation has reached high levels across the developed world, where economies in North America, Europe, and Asia now seem at risk of stagnation. A glance at the history of publishing in management education would suggest that all the aforementioned represent topics which management educators might investigate.

However, in considering possibilities for devising research agendas around the beliefs, practices, institutions, and social relations of the intellectual field of management education, it would seem there are other possibilities for scholars to make their mark. While management education journals are full of research related to trends, it is hoped this book has encouraged scholars to consider how research agendas might be pursued by turning the focus of attention back in on management education itself.

The argument made here is that the best way to advance the future of management education research is by developing scholars who take a fascination in the subject. The suggestion is that the quality scholarship in this intellectual field will come from management educators who better understand themselves and locate their scholarly approach within the tradition to which they wish to contribute. For this purpose, the reader has been introduced to three schools of management education, the Rational School, the Critical School, and the Postliberal School.

Identified above are challenges for the Rational School in the apparent erosion of its eminent position in the publishing field, as well as ongoing links between management education and the corporation, and how pedagogy might stay in advance of market-based educational needs. In light of these issues, Rational scholars might be well placed to pursue research agendas based on the relationship between rational pragmatism and scientific empiricism, links between micro-based action and macro-based societal change, and how skills-based education can keep in advance of corporate interests.

Challenges for Critical scholars include the monetisation by corporations of identity-based Critical endeavours, the retreat from all forms of authority except that of the teacher, and the rise of Critical scholarship to a seeming eminence in the publishing field while portraying themselves as rebel outsiders. Suggested topics of interest therefore include investigation of the nature of radicalism in management education, the relationship between authority and the teacher, and issues of cognitive dissonance.

The Postliberal scholar faces circumstances of preserving a traditional approach to management education, while also having limited access to regular scholarly publishing outlets and finding few like-minded persons within the intellectual field. Such management educators might therefore explore topics related to issues of tradition within management education, understanding the possibilities inherent to other forms of publishing, and techniques for building up a scholarly community.

Scholars of all stripes might like to consider issues related to differentiation between the leading journals of management education, and the seeming trend towards special issues. Interested parties could also consider issues related to greater originality in scholarship. Such a research programme might include more formal analyses of that which is published, in order to establish emerging themes. Furthermore, there is opportunity to consider how teaching practice reflects a diagonalisation of all of the schools of management education, where we take not one approach but the best parts of each of the three.

If there is one summarising thought I would offer at the end of this book, it would therefore be a call for us to consider more often focusing on the intellectual field of management education itself – how it is developing, and how it might develop. In the rush to investigate trends, there seem to be engaging and interesting questions we may overlook, or never even ask. While there is probably no end to the number of themes which could be investigated in the area of management education itself, hopefully you have found motivation in some of the suggestions provided here.

It is my belief that we owe it to those management educators who have come before us, and those who will come after us, to engage in this introspection. In the Preface to this book, I mentioned the *Far Side* cartoon I sent to Dallas Hanson just prior to his passing. In the cartoon, a man named Darrell is staring at his reflection in the spoon using the concave side. The caption is, 'someone had once again slipped him [Darrell] a spoon with the concave side reversed' (Larson, 2023). Just as the concave side of the spoon provided Darrell with a different view of himself, my hope is that this book has also helped you as a management educator to see yourself and your intellectual field in a different light. If you ask questions of yourself, and your field, my view is that such a practice has every likelihood of serving as the basis for an enjoyable and rewarding career in advancing the future of management education research.

References

Adair, P., Adair, N., Brown, A., Epstein, R., Phenix, L.M., & Selver, V. (Directors). (1977). *Word Is Out: Stories of some of our lives.* [Film]. Mariposa Film Group.

Adams, J.D. (1977). A Program for Improving the Management Of Stress. *The Teaching of Organizational Behavior*, 2(4), 17–22.

Aguilar, F. (1967). *Scanning the Business Environment.* Macmillan.

Akin, G. (1979). An Exercise in Social Power. *Exchange: The Organizational Behavior Teaching Journal*, 3(4), 38–39.

Akin, G. (1984) Thoughts About Authority and the Experiential Teacher. *Organizational Behavior Teaching Review*, 9(1), 65–69.

Akin, G. (1991). Self-Directed Learning in Introductory Management. *Journal of Management Education*, 15(3), 295–312.

Akin, G. (1995). Racy Talk at Work. *Management Learning*, 26(4), 483–492.

Akin, G. (2000). Learning About Work From Joe Cool. *Journal of Management Inquiry*, 9(1), 57–61.

Allan, B. (2007). Time To Learn? E-Learners' experiences of time in virtual learning communities. *Management Learning*, 38(5), 557–572.

Allan, G. (2012). *Modes of Learning: Whitehead's metaphysics and the stages of education.* SUNY Press.

Allcot, D. (2021, 24 April). *A Look at Caitlyn Jenner's Net Worth as She Runs for Governor of California.* Yahoo! Finance. https:// finance .yahoo .com/ news/ look -caitlyn -jenner -net -worth -194000248 .html ?guccounter = 1 & guce _referrer = a HR0cHM6Ly9 3d3cuZ29vZ 2xlLmNvbS8 & guce _referrer _sig = AQAAAKG3 wfSF7dutK1 crPYMIBRQh kB7jAMSFec kQGWFCIyrN rJrjPtv2Rc wqeXuyVX2V _Scq0fRBhFuzHHcL -E4Tgk jG6lF4aWmg gLdaTS2ZJC foWME2zUdD YSBVmkxJnN-m-8uM_kgzbzud9PFW56wE5L7axxSMXvrjB_mv-rXPDDr0

Allen, S.J. (2020). On the Cutting Edge or the Chopping Block? Fostering a digital mindset and tech literacy in business management education. *Journal of Management Education*, 44(3), 362–393.

Alsop, R.J. (2006). Business Ethics Education in Business Schools: A commentary. *Journal of Management Education*, 30(1), 11–14.

Alvesson, M., & Willmott, H. (1992). On the Idea of Emancipation in Management and Organization Studies. *Academy of Management Review*, 17(3), 432–454.

Amdam, R.P., & Benito, G.R.G. (2022). Opening the Black Box of International Strategy Formation: How Harvard Business School became a multinational enterprise. *Academy of Management Learning and Education*, 21(2), 167–187.

Anderson, C. (2016). *White Rage: The unspoken truth of our racial divide.* Bloomsbury.

Anderson, L., Thorpe, R., & Coleman, C. (2020). Reviewing Management Learning: The field and the journal. *Management Learning*, 51(1), 17 34.

Apple. (2023, 19 January). *In Celebration of Black History Month, Apple Releases New Black Unity Collection and Content.* Apple. https://www.apple.com/au/newsroom/ 2023/01/apple-celebrates-Black-history-month-with-unity-collection-and-exclusive -content/

Athos, A.G. (1979). Contingencies Beyond Reasoning. *Exchange: The Organizational Behavior Teaching Journal*, 4(2), 7–12.

Audebrand, L.K., & Pepin, M. (2022). Principles for Responsible Management Education: An axiological approach. *Journal of Management Education*, 46(5), 888–919.

Augier, M. (2004). James March on Education, Leadership and Don Quixote: Introduction and interview. *Academy of Management Learning and Education*, 3(2), 169–177.

Azevedo, G. (2023). Into the Realm of Organizational Folly: A poem, a review, and a typology of organizational stupidity. *Management Learning*, 54(2), 267–281.

Baddeley, S., & James, K. (1987). Owl, Fox, Donkey or Sheep: Political skills for managers. *Management Education and Development*, 18(1), 3–19.

Bakir, V. (2006). Greenpeace v Shell: Media exploitation and the social amplification of risk framework (SARF). *Journal of Risk Research*, 8(7–8), 679–691.

Ballinger, F. (1991–1992). Ambigere: The Euro-American picaro and the Native American trickster. *MELUS*, 17(1), 21–38.

Bamber, M., Allen-Collinson, J., & McCormack, J. (2017). Occupational Limbo, Transitional Liminality and Permanent Liminality: New conceptual distinctions. *Human Relations*, 70(12), 1514–1537.

Banerjee, S.B. (2011). Embedding Sustainability Across the Organization: A critical perspective. *Academy of Management Learning and Education*, 10(4), 719–731.

Barney, J. (1991). Firm Resources and Sustained Competitive Advantage. *Journal of Management*, 17(1), 99–120.

Barry, D., & Elmes, M. (1997). Strategy Retold: Toward a narrative view of strategic discourse. *Academy of Management Review*, 22(2), 429–452.

Barry, D., & Meisiek, S. (2015). Discovering the Business Studio. *Journal of Management Education*, 39(1), 153–175.

Bartolome, F. (1990). The Problems of a Man Teaching Some Women About Women. *Organizational Behavior Teaching Review*, 14(1), 44–51.

Bartz, D.E., Hillman, L.W., Lehrer, S., & Mayhugh, G.M. (1990). A Model for Managing Workforce Diversity. *Management Education and Development*, 21(5), 321–326.

Bass, D. (2020, 23 June). *Microsoft to Add US$150m on Diversity, Double Black Leaders*. Bloomberg News. https://www.bnnbloomberg.ca/microsoft-to-add-150-million-on-diversity-double-Black-leaders-1.1454963

Bauer-Wolf, J. (2018, 22 February). *Overconfident Students, Dubious Employers*. Inside Higher Ed. https://www.insidehighered.com/news/2018/02/23/study-students-believe-they-are-prepared-workplace-employers-disagree

Beatty, J.E., Leigh, J.S.A., & Dean, K.L. (2009). Philosophy Rediscovered: Exploring the connections between teaching philosophies, educational philosophies, and philosophy. *Journal of Management Education*, 33(1), 99–114.

Bell, D. (1971). The Corporation and Society in the 1970s. *The Public Interest*, 24(Summer), 5.

Bell, E., & King, D. (2010). The Elephant in the Room. *Management Learning*, 41(4), 429–442.

Bell, E.S. (1988). The Clash of World Views in John Kennedy Toole's *A Confederacy of Dunces'*. *The Southern Literary Journal*, 21(1), 15–22.

Berger, P.L., Berger, B., & Kellner, H. (1973). *The Homeless Mind: Modernization and consciousness*. Penguin Books.

Bergman, J.Z., Westerman, J.W., & Daly, J.P. (2010). Narcissism in Management Education. *Academy of Management Learning and Education*, 9(1), 119–131.

Bergman, J.Z., Westerman, J.W., Bergman, S.M., Westerman, J., & Daly, J.P. (2014). Narcissism, Materialism, and Environmental Ethics in Business Students. *Journal of Management Education*, 38(4), 489–510.

Berry, W. (2000). *What Are People For?* North Point Press.

Berry, W. (2010). *The Hidden Wound*. Counterpoint.

Berry, W. (2015). *The Unsettling of America: Culture and agriculture*. Counterpoint.

Berry, W. (2018). *The World-Ending Fire: The essential Wendell Berry*. Penguin Press.

Best, S., & Kellner, D. (1991). *Postmodern Theory: Critical interrogations*. Guilford.

Bigelow, J. (1986). Using Microcomputers in Teaching OB. *Organizational Behavior Teaching Review*, 10(4), 71–86.

Bilimioria, D. (1997). Management Educators: In danger of becoming pedestrians on the information superhighway. *Journal of Management Education*, 21(2), 232–243.

Bilimoria, D. (1998). From Classroom Learning to Real-World Learning: A diasporic shift in management education. *Journal of Management Education*, 22(3), 265–268.

Bilimoria, D. (1999). Emerging Information Technologies and Management Education. *Journal of Management Education*, 23(3), 229–232.

Bittner, E. (1965). The Concept of Organization. *Social Research*, 32(3), 239–255.

Blackman, D., Kennedy, M., & Quazi, A. (2013). Corporate Social Responsibility and Individual Resistance: Learning as the missing link in implementation. *Management Learning*, 44(3), 237–252.

Blank, S. (2013). Why the Lean Start-Up Changes Everything. *Harvard Business Review*, 91(5), 63–72.

Blond, P. (2010). *Red Tory: How left and right have broken Britain and how we can fix it*. Faber.

Boddy, D., & Buchanan, D. (1984). Implications for Development of New Technology. *Management Education and Development*, 15(2), 176–182.

Boeble, H.K., & Buchanan, P.J. (1975). A Module on What the Manager Does. *The Teaching of Organizational Behavior*, 1(4), 29–32.

Boje, D.M. (1995). Stories of the Storytelling Organization: A postmodern analysis of Disney as 'Tamara-Land'. *Academy of Management Journal*, 38(4), 997–1035.

Boje, D.M. (2001). *Narrative Methods for Organizational and Communication Research*. Sage Publications.

Bolinger, A.R., & Brown, K.D. (2014). Entrepreneurial Failure as a Threshold Concept: The effects of student experiences. *Journal of Management Education*, 39(4), 452–475.

Bolman, L., & Deal, T.E. (2017). Power and the Power Simulation: Then and now. *Journal of Management Education*, 41(5), 627–633.

Bolton, R. (1975). Plato's Distinction Between Being and Becoming. *The Review of Metaphysics*, 29(1), 66–95.

Bourdieu, P. (1969). Intellectual Field and Creative Project. *Social Science Information*, 8(2), 89–119.

Boyatzis, R.E. (1994). Stimulating Self-Directed Learning Through the Managerial Assessment and Development Course. *Journal of Management Education*, 18(3), 304–323.

Boyer, E.L. (1990). *Scholarship Reconsidered: Priorities of the Professoriate*. Princeton University Press.

Bradford, D.L. (1975a). Editorial Statement. *The Teaching of Organization Behavior*, 1(1), 2.

Bradford, D.L. (1975b). Editorial Statement. *The Teaching of Organization Behavior*, 1(2), 2–3.

Brady, F.N. (1990). Detached Intellectuals and Moral Activists. *Organizational Behavior Teaching Review*, 14(3), 23–26.

Brannen, T.R. (1986). New Directions For Business Education. *Organizational Behavior Teaching Review*, 10(2), 1–10.

Bridgman, T., Cummings, S., & Ballard, J. (2019). Who Built Maslow's Pyramid? A history of the creation of management studies' most famous symbol and its implications for management education. *Academy of Management Learning and Education*, 18(1), 81–98.

Bridgman, T., Cummings, S., & McLaughlin, C. (2016). Restating the Case: How revisiting the development of the case method can help us think differently about the future of the business school. *Academy of Management Learning and Education*, 15(4), 724–741.

Bristow, A., Robinson, S., & Ratle, O. (2017). Being an Early-Career CMS Academic in the Context of Insecurity and 'Excellence': The dialectics of resistance and compliance. *Organization Studies*, 38(9), 1185–1207.

Bristow, A., Robinson, S., & Ratle, O. (2019). Academic Arrhythmia: Disruption, dissonance and conflict in the early-career rhythms of CMS academics. *Academy of Management Learning and Education*, 18(2), 241–260.

Brontë, C. (1847). *Jane Eyre: An autobiography*. Smith, Elder & Co.

Brown, N. (1979). The Management of Diversity: Or why include sexism and racism as topics in executive development programs. *Exchange: The Organizational Behavior Teaching Journal*, 4(4), 19–22.

Burleigh, N. (2015, 28 January). What Silicon Valley Thinks of Women. *Newsweek*. https://www.newsweek.com/2015/02/06/what-silicon-valley-thinks-women-302821.html

Burns, T., & Stalker, G.M. (1961). *The Management of Innovation*. Tavistock.

Burton, B.K., & Dunn, C.P. (2005). The Caring Approach and Social Issues in Management Education. *Journal of Management Education*, 29(3), 453–474.

Burton, B.K., Dunn, C.P., & Goldsby, M. (2006). Moral Pluralism in Business Ethics Education: It's about time. *Journal of Management Education*, 30(1), 90–105.

Butler, J. (2004). *Undoing Gender*. Routledge.

Byrne, A., Crossan, M., & Seijts, G. (2018). The Development of Leader Character Through Crucible Moments. *Journal of Management Education*, 42(2), 265–293.

Cabantous, L., Gond, J.P., Harding, N., & Learmonth, M. (2015). Critical Essay: Reconsidering critical performativity. *Human Relations*, 69(2), 197–213.

Calhoun, C.J. (1983). The Radicalism of Tradition: Community strength or venerable disguise and borrowed language? *American Journal of Sociology*, 88(5), 886–914.

Calkins, R.D. (1946). Objectives of Business Education. *Harvard Business Review*, 25(1), 46–57.

Calvard, T.S. (2016). Big Data, Organizational Learning, and Sensemaking: Theorizing interpretive challenges under conditions of dynamic complexity. *Management Learning*, 47(1), 65–82.

Cameron, K.S., Ireland, R.D., Lussier, R.N., New, J.R., & Robbins, S.P. (2003). Management Textbooks as Propaganda. *Journal of Management Education*, 27(6), 711–729.

Caputo, R.K. (2002). Social Justice, the Ethics of Care, and Market Economies. *Families in Society*, 83(4), 355–364.

Carlin, M. (2021a). Augusto Del Noce: Toward an education of limits. *Educational Theory*, 71(5), 631–650.

Carlin, M. (2021b). Gnosticism, Progressivism and the (Im)possibility of the Ethical Academy. *Educational, Philosophy and Theory*, 53(5), 436–447.

Carter, P., & Jackson, N. (1990). The Emergence of Postmodern Management? *Management Education and Development*, 21(3), 219–228.

Carter, W.R. (2023). Tackling Weaknesses in Students' Financial Analysis Capabilities: A value-based exercise for strategic management courses. *Management Teaching Review*, 8(1), 57–67.

Case, P., & Selvester, K. (2000). Close Encounters: Ideological invasion and complicity on an 'International Management' master's programme. *Management Learning*, 31(1), 11–23.

Cave, N., & O'Hagan (2022). *Faith, Hope and Carnage*. Text Publishing Company.

Caza, A. (2020). The Gig Economy's Implications for Management Education. *Journal of Management Education*, 44(5), 594–604.

Chandler, G. (1979). The Manager as a Political Animal. *Management Education and Development*, 10(3), 191–193.

Chang, J., & Rieple, A. (2018). Entrepreneurial Decision-Making in a Microcosm. *Management Learning*, 49(4), 471–497.

Chiles, T.H. (2003). Process Theorizing: Too important to ignore in a kaleidic world. *Academy of Management Learning and Education*, 2(3), 288–291.

Clawson, J.G., & Doner, J. (1996). Teaching Leadership Through Aikido. *Journal of Management Education*, 20(2), 182–205.

Clegg, S., Pina e Cunha, M., Rego, A., & Berti, M. (2022). Speaking Truth to Power: The academic as jester stimulating management learning. *Management Learning*, 53(3), 547–565.

Clegg, S., Pitelis, C., Schweitzer, J., & Whittle, A. (2023). *Strategy: Theory and practice*. Sage Publications.

Cohen, A.R. (1975). A Funny Thing Happened on the Way From the Theater: An involved spectator's notes on teaching by play-going. *The Teaching of Organizational Behavior*, 1(3), 2–7.

Cohen, A.R. (1976). Beyond Simulation: Treating the classroom as an organization. *The Teaching of Organizational Behavior*, 2(1), 13–19.

Cohen, A.R., & Miaoulis, G. (1978). MBA Student Anxiety and Overreactions: Learning from linking the required OB and Marketing courses. *Exchange: The Organizational Behavior Teaching Journal*, 3(2), 11–15.

Cohen, D.J., & Lippert, S.K. (1999). The Lure of Technology: Panacea or pariah? *Journal of Management Education*, 23(6), 743–746.

Colby, A., Ehrlich, T., Sullivan, W.M., & Dolle, J.R. (2011). *Rethinking Undergraduate Business Education: Liberal learning for the profession*. Jossey-Bass.

Collins, D. (1996). Distributive Justice and Capitalism: A Rawlsian exercise. *Journal of Management Education*, 20(1), 82–86.

Collins, D. (1999). The Dollar Game: Questioning the ethics of capitalism and bargaining. *Journal of Management Education*, 23(3), 302–310.

Comer, D.R., & Cooper, E.A. (1998). Gender Relations and Sexual Harassment in the Workplace: Michael Crichton's *Disclosure* as a teaching tool. *Journal of Management Education*, 22(2), 227–241.

Comer, D.R., & Schwartz, M. (2020). Adapting Mussar to Develop Management Students' Character. *Journal of Management Education*, 44(2), 196–246.

Comte, T.E. (1980). Improving Oral Presentation Skills Using Videotape: A strategic management course experience. *Exchange: The Organizational Behavior Teaching Journal*, 5(4), 27–29.

Crossman, J. (2015). Manager Perspectives on Embedding Workplace Spirituality into the Business Curriculum: Bridging the gap. *Thunderbird International Business Review*, 57(5), 367–378.

Cummings, L. (1990). Reflections on Management Education and Development: Drift or thrust into the 21st century? *Academy of Management Review*, 15(4), 694–696.

Cummings, S., & Bridgman, T. (2011). The Relevant Past: Why the history of management should be critical for our future. *Academy of Management Learning and Education*, 10(1), 77–93.

Cunliffe, A.L. (2004). On Becoming a Critically Reflexive Practitioner. *Journal of Management Education*, 28(4), 407–426.

Cunningham, I. (1981). Management Development and Women. *Management Education and Development*, 12(1), 5–14.

Dahl, R. (1988). *Matilda*. Jonathan Cape.

Daspit, J.J., & D'Souza, D.E. (2012). Using the Community of Inquiry Framework to Introduce Wiki Environments in Blended-Learning Pedagogies: Evidence from a business capstone course. *Academy of Management Learning and Education*, 11(4), 666–683.

Dauncey, G. (1988*). After the Crash*. Marshall, Morgan & Scott.

David, L., & Seinfeld, J. (Creators). (1989–1998). *Seinfeld*. [TV series]. NBC.

Davies, J. (1985). Why Are Women Not Where the Power Is? An examination of the maintenance of power elites. *Management Education and Development*, 16(3), 278–288.

De Cervantes, M. (1605). *Don Quixote*. Francisco de Robles.

De Haan, E., Bertie, C., Day, A., & Sills, C. (2010). Clients' Critical Moments of Coaching: Toward a 'client model' of executive coaching. *Academy of Management Learning and Education*, 9(4), 607–621.

Dean, K.L. (2018). Academic Gerrymandering? Expansion and expressions of academic work. *Journal of Management Inquiry*, 27(4), 405–410.

Dean, K.L., & Beggs, J.M. (2006). University Professors and Teaching Ethics: Conceptualizations and expectations. *Journal of Management Education*, 30(1), 15–44.

Del Noce, A., & Lancellotti, C. (2015). *The Crisis of Modernity*. McGill-Queen's University Press.

Del Noce, A., & Lancellotti, C. (2017). *The Age of Secularization*. McGill-Queen's University Press.

Delbecq, A. (2000). Spirituality for Business Leadership. Reporting on a pilot course for MBAs and CEOs. *Journal of Management Inquiry*, 9(2), 117–128.

Deneen, P.J. (2018). *Why Liberalism Failed*. Yale University Press.

Deneen, P.J. (2022, 23 April). *The Unholy Marriage of Marx and Ayn Rand*. Compact. https://compactmag.com/article/the-unholy-marriage-of-marx-and-ayn-rand

Dent, E.B. (2000). The Unique Governance Challenge of Graduate Contract-Cohort Programs. *Journal of Management Education*, 24(1), 55–72.

Dent, E.B. (2002). The Messy History of OB&D: How three strands came to be seen as one rope. *Journal of Management History*, 40(3), 266–280.

Dent, E.B. (2017). Jerry Harvey: The quintessential life of sense and nonsense. *Journal of Management, Spirituality & Religion*, 14(2), 109–116.

Dent, E.B. (2022). A Paean to the 'Poet Laureate of Management' Peter B Vaill. In S.K. Dhiman & J.F. Marques (eds), *Leadership After COVID-19: Working together toward a sustainable future* (pp.31–45). Springer.

Dewey, J. (1922). *Human Nature and Conduct: An introduction to social psychology.* Henry Holt and Company.

Dewey, J. (1929). *The Quest For Certainty.* George Allen & Unwin Ltd.

Dewey, J. (1930). *Human Nature and Conduct: An introduction to social psychology.* The Macmillan Company.

Dobson, J., & White, J. (1995). Toward the Feminine Firm: An extension to Thomas White. *Business Ethics Quarterly*, 5(3), 463–478.

Dodd, T., Graves, C., & Hentzen, J. (2022). Impact and University Business Training Courses Delivered to the Marginalized: A systematic review. *Academy of Management Learning and Education*, 21(3), 449–469.

Dodge, L.D. (1980). Deterministic Illusion in the Organizational Sciences: Service or sabotage? *Exchange: The Organizational Behavior Teaching Journal*, 5(3), 29–32.

Donaldson-Feilder, E., Lewis, R., Yarker, J., & Whiley, L.A. (2022). Interpersonal Mindfulness in Leadership Development: A Delphi study. *Journal of Management Education*, 46(5), 816–852.

Doucette, M.B., Gladstone, J.S., & Carter, T. (2021). Indigenous Conversational Approach to History and Business Education. *Academy of Management Learning and Education*, 20(3), 473–484.

Dreher, R. (2019). *The Benedict Option: A strategy for Christians in a post-Christian nation.* Sentinel.

DuBrin, A.J. (1992). Computer-Assisted Scenario Analysis (CASA): Using word processing to enhance case analysis. *Journal of Management Education*, 16(3), 385–390.

Duncan, W.J. (1986). Focussing on the MBA Purpose Rather Than the MBA End. *Organizational Behavior Teaching Review*, 10(1), 71–73.

Durbrow, B.R. (1978). An Exercise on the Impact of Leadership Style and Job Design on Worker Motivation. *Exchange: The Organizational Behavior Teaching Journal*, 3(2), 32–33.

Dyer, R.F. (1987). An Integrated Design for Personal Computers in the Marketing Curriculum. *Journal of the Academy of Marketing Sciences*, 15(Summer), 16–24.

Edmondson, B.S., Edmondson, V.C., Adams, J., & Barnes, J. (2020). We Challenge You to Join the Movement: From discourse to critical voice. *Journal of Management Education*, 44(2), 247–266.

Edwards, M.S., & Leigh, J.S.A. (2022). Getting Published in JME: Top 10 tips from the co-editors. *Journal of Management Education*, 46(1), 3–15.

Egri, C.P. (1999). The Environmental Round Table Role-Playing Exercise: The dynamics of multistakeholder decision-making processes. *Journal of Management Education*, 23(1), 95–112.

Endrissat, N. (2021). Book Review: *The Robotic Imaginary. The human and the price of dehumanized labor. Management Learning*, 52(2), 259–262.

Erdynast, A. (1990). Commentary on 'Teaching Ethics Means Practicing Ethics: When a student says his company is breaking the law'. *Organizational Behavior Teaching Review*, 14(3), 32–37.

Eriksen, M., Cooper, K., & Miccolis, A. (2019). On Becoming Virtuous. *Journal of Management Education*, 43(6), 630–650.

ESPN (2021, 23 June). *Las Vegas Raiders DE Carl Nassib Has Top-Selling NFL Jersey at Fanatics in Day Since Announcement.* ESPN. https://www.espn.com.au/nfl/story/

_/id/31688171/las-vegas-raiders-de-carl-nassib-top-selling-nfl-jersey-fanatics-day-announcement

Evans, M.D. (1998). *Whitehead and Philosophy of Education: The seamless coat of learning*. Rodopi.

Farrell, G. (2021, 24 May). *Bill Gates' Long History of Problematic Behavior With Women Is Being Revealed*. Evie. https://www.eviemagazine.com/post/bill-gates-long-history-of-problematic-behavior-with-women-is-being-revealed

Fay, B. (1987). *Critical Social Science*. Polity Press.

Feldman, M., & Worline, M. (2016). The Practicality of Practice Theory. *Academy of Management Learning and Education*, 15(2), 304–324.

Fenn, M. (1978). *Making It in Management: A behavioural approach for women executives*. Prentice Hall.

Ferdinand, J. (2004). Power, Politics and State Intervention in Organizational Learning. *Management Learning*, 35(4), 435–450.

Ferraro, H.S. (2023). Disrupting Dominant Narratives and Privilege: Teaching Black women's enterprise and activism. *Journal of Management Education*, 47(1), 40–55.

Ferris, W.P. (1996). The Effectiveness of Teaching Business Ethics Using Moral Philosophy and Personal Ethical Codes. *Journal of Management Education*, 20(3), 341–357.

Fink, S. (1979). A Conversation With Tony Athos. *Exchange: The Organizational Behavior Teaching Journal*, 4(4), 5–11.

Flexner, A. (1930). *Universities: American, English, German*. Oxford University Press.

Flyvbjerg, B. (2001). *Making Social Science Matter*. Cambridge University Press.

Fonda, N. (1979). Book Reviews: *Making It in Management: A behavioural approach for women executives*. *Management Education and Development*, 10(3), 229–230.

Foote, L.M. (2013). Honing Crisis Communication Skills: Using interactive media and student-centered learning to develop agile leaders. *Journal of Management Education*, 37(1), 79–114.

Forray, J.M., & Dean, K.L. (2016). Welcome to Management Teaching Review! *Management Teaching Review*, 1(1), 4–6.

Forray, J.M., & Leigh, J.S.A. (2012). A Primer on the Principles of Responsible Management Education: Intellectual roots and waves of change. *Journal of Management Education*, 36(3), 295–309.

Forray, J.M., Leigh, J.S.A., & Kenworthy, A.L. (2015). Special Section Cluster on Responsible Management Education: Nurturing an emerging PRME ethos. *Academy of Management Learning and Education*, 14(2), 293–296.

Fortune (2000, 14 May). Fortune 500 2000. https://fortune.com/ranking/fortune500/2000/

Foster, J., Helms Mills, J., & Mills, A.J. (2014). Shades of Red: Cold War influences on Canadian and US Business Textbooks. *Journal of Management Education*, 38(5), 642–671.

Foster, W.M. (2020). From the Editors – Extending the Big Table: A call to action. *Academy of Management Learning and Education*, 19(4), 435–438.

Fotaki, M., & Prasad, A. (2015). Questioning Neoliberal Capitalism and Economic Inequality in Business Schools. *Academy of Management Learning and Education*, 14(4), 556–575.

Foucault, M. (1977). *Discipline and Punish*. Penguin.

Fougere, M., & Moulettes, A. (2011). Disclaimers, Dichotomies and Disappearances in International Business Textbooks: A postcolonial deconstruction. *Management Learning*, 43(1), 5–24.

Fox, S. (2009). 'This Interpreted World': Two turns to the social in management learning. *Management Learning*, 40(4), 371–378.

Fox, S., & Moult, G. (1990). Postmodern Culture and Management Development. *Management Education and Development*, 21(3), 168–170.

Freeman, R.E. (1984). *Strategic Management: A stakeholder approach*. Pitman.

Freire, P. (1972). *Pedagogy of the Oppressed*. Penguin.

Freire, P. (2021). *Education for Critical Consciousness*. Bloomsbury Collections.

French, J.R.P., & Raven, B. (1959). The Bases of Social Power. In D. Cartwright & A. Zander (eds), *Group Dynamics* (pp. 150–167). Harper and Row.

Friedland, J., & Jain, T. (2020). Reframing the Purpose of Business Education: Crowding-in a culture of moral self-awareness. *Journal of Management Inquiry*, 31(1), 15–29.

Friedman, M. (1970, 13 September). A Friedman-Doctrine: The social responsibility of business is to increase its profits. *The New York Times*, 17.

Friedman, M. (2002). *Capitalism and Freedom* (40th anniversary edition). University of Chicago Press.

Fromm, E. (1941). *The Fear of Freedom*. Routledge & Kegan Paul.

Fromm, E. (1960). *Escape From Freedom*. Routledge.

Fukami, C.V. (2002). 9/11 Montage: Professors remember. *Academy of Management Learning and Education*, 1(1), 38–54.

Fukami, C.V. (2007). The Third Road. *Journal of Management Education*, 31(3), 358–364.

Fukami, C.V., Allen, D.B., & Wittmer, D.P. (2022). Teaching Management in the Fourth Industrial Revolution. In M.R. Fellenz, S. Hoidn, & M. Brady (eds), *The Future of Management Education* (pp. 153–171). Routledge.

Garratt, R. (1972). Towards a Reform of Management Education. *Management Education and Development*, 3(1), 3–7.

Gerard, J.G. (2012). Linking in With LinkedIn: Three exercises that enhance professional social networking and career building. *Journal of Management Education*, 36(6), 866–897.

Gherardi, S., & Murgia, A. (2015). Imagine Being Asked to Evaluate Your CEO …: Using the constructive controversy approach to teach gender and management in times of economic crisis. *Management Learning*, 46(1), 6–23.

Ghoshal, S. (2003, 17 July). Business Schools Share the Blame for Enron. *Financial Times*, 21.

Ghoshal, S. (2005). Bad Management Theories Are Destroying Good Management Practices. *Academy of Management Learning and Education*, 4(1), 75–91.

Giacalone, R.A. (2007). Taking a Red Pill to Disempower Unethical Students: Creating ethical sentinels in business schools. *Academy of Management Learning and Education*, 6(4), 534–542.

Giacalone, R.A., & Thompson, K. (2006). Business Ethics and Social Responsibility Education: Shifting the worldview. *Academy of Management Learning and Education*, 5(3), 266–277.

Glaser, B., & Strauss, A. (1999). *Discovery of Grounded Theory: Strategies for qualitative research*. Routledge.

Goelz, P.C. (1958). Toward a Concept of Education for Administration. *The Journal of the Academy of Management*, 1(1), 62–63.

Gordon, A. (1978). Star Wars: A myth for our time. *Literature/Film Quarterly*, 6(4), 314–326.

Gordon, R.A., & Howell, J.E. (1959). *Higher Education for Business*. Columbia University Press.

Greenberg, D.N., & Hibbert, P. (2022). Beyond Legitimacy: A bold agenda for MLE Scholarship. *Academy of Management Learning and Education*, 21(2), 161–166.

Greenberg, D.N., Clair, J.A., & Maclean, T.L., (2002). Teaching Through Traumatic Events: Uncovering the choices of management educators as they responded to September 11th. *Academy of Management Learning and Education*, 1(1), 38–54.

Guest, R.H. (1976). Teaching OB Through Field Research and Consultation Projects. *The Teaching of Organizational Behavior*, 2(1), 25–29.

Hadjimichael, D., & Tsoukas, H. (2023). Phronetic Improvisation: A virtue ethics perspective. *Management Learning*, 54(1), 99–120.

Hahn, C., & Vignon, C. (2019). Management Education From Episteme to Phronesis: The contribution of French didactic theory. *Management Learning*, 50(3), 337–354.

Hai, D.M. (1982). Teaching 'Women in Management' Courses: Current issues. *Exchange: The Organizational Behavior Teaching Journal*, 7(4), 38–40.

Haire, A.J. (1928). We Make Our Bow. *The Business School Journal*, 1(1), 5.

Hall, J.C. (1996), Creating Materials for Interactive Television ('Winging It' Doesn't Work). *Journal of Management Education*, 20(3), 386–398.

Halliday, J., & Johnsson, M. (2009). A MacIntyrian Perspective on Organizational Learning. *Management Learning*, 41(1), 37–51.

Hamdani, M. (2021). A Multi-Skill, 5-Week, Online Positive Emotions Training for Student Well-Being. *Journal of Management Education*, 45(1), 86–125.

Hamdani, M., Wallin, A., Ashkanasy, N.M., & Fenton-O'Creevy, M. (2023). Common Methodological Issues in Quantitative Management Education Research and Recommendation for Authors. *Journal of Management Education*. Online First.

Hamilton, D., McFarland, D., & Mirchamdani, D. (2000). A Decision Model for Integration Across the Business Curriculum in the 21st Century. *Journal of Management Education*, 24(1), 102–126.

Hammond, V., & Boydell, T. (1985). Men and Women in Organisations: The issues. *Management Education and Development*, 16(2), 77–78.

Handy, C.B. (1975). The Contrasting Philosophies of Management Education. *Management Education and Development*, 6(2), 56–62.

Handy, C.B. (1977). 'Is This the Way to the Future?' A personal view of the management education scene. *Management Education and Development*, 8, 57–62.

Hannah, D.R., & Robertson, K.M. (2016). Jarvis Manufacturing: An experiential exercise for teaching the fundamentals of teamwork. *Management Teaching Review*, 1(1), 7–18.

Hanson, D., Steen, J., & Liesch, P.W. (1997). Reluctance to Innovate: A case study of the titanium dioxide industry. *Premetheus*, 15(3), 345–356.

Harley, B. (2019). Confronting the Crisis of Confidence in Management Studies: Why senior scholars need to stop setting a bad example. *Academy of Management Learning and Education*, 18(2), 286–297.

Harney, S., & Linstead, S.A. (2009). Faith and Fortune in the Post-Colonial Classroom. *Management Learning*, 40(1), 69–85.

Harrison, R. (1973). Towards a Strategy for Helping Redundant and Retiring Managers. *Management Education and Development*, 4(2), 77–85.

Hartman, E.M. (2006). Can We Teach Character? An Aristotelian answer. *Academy of Management Learning and Education*, 5(1), 68–81.

Harvey, J.B. (1977). Organizations as Phrog Farms. *Organizational Dynamics*, 5(4), 15–23.

Harvey, J.B. (1979). Learning To Not Teach. *Exchange: The Organizational Behavior Teaching Journal*, 4(2), 19–21.

Harvey, J.B. (1984). Encouraging Students to Cheat: One thought on the difference between teaching ethics and teaching ethically. *Organizational Behavior Teaching Review*, 9(2), 1–13.

Harvey, J.B. (1988). *The Abilene Paradox and Other Meditations on Management*. Lexington Books.

Harvey, J.B. (1999). *How Come Every Time I Get Stabbed in the Back My Fingerprints Are on the Knife? And other meditations on management*. Jossey-Bass.

Hayek, F.A.v. (1942). Scientism and the Study of Society. *Economica*, 9(35), 267–291.

Hedberg, P.R. (2009). Learning Through Reflective Classroom Practice: Applications to educate the reflective manager. *Journal of Management Education*, 33(1), 10–36.

Henderson, A. (1973). Critical Comments on the Allen Approach. *Management Education and Development*, 4(1), 32–36.

Hennessey, J.W. (1980). The Place of Values in Teaching Organizational Behavior. *Exchange: The Organizational Behavior Teaching Journal*, 5(1), 3–4.

Herring, R.A., & Mendleson, J.L. (1999). Use of a Student Ombudsperson to Enhance Communication in University Classes. *Journal of Management Education*, 23(5), 574–583.

Hibbert, P. (2018). From the AMLE Editorial Team: Disciplined provocation: Writing essays for AMLE. *Academy of Management Learning and Education*, 17(4), 397–400.

Hibbert, P., Beech, N., & Siedlok, F. (2018). Leadership Formation: Interpreting experience. *Academy of Management Learning and Education*, 16(4), 603–622.

Hietanen, J., & Mohammed, S. (2023). Is It All Just Melancholic Pedagogy? Accelerationism and the future of critical management education. *Management Learning*.

Hjorth, D. (2003). In the Tribe of Sisyphus: Rethinking management education from an 'entrepreneurial' perspective. *Journal of Management Education*, 27(6), 637–653.

Hochschild, J.P. (2020, 5 August). *Race and Anti-Fragility: Wendell Berry's 'The Hidden Wound' at fifty*. Commonweal. https://www.commonwealmagazine.org/race-anti-fragility

Holmer, L.L. (2014). Understanding and Reducing the Impact of Defensiveness on Management Learning: Some lessons from neuroscience. *Journal of Management Education*, 38(5), 618–641.

Homer. (1919). *The Odyssey*. W. Heinemann.

Hope, R.P., & Higgins, J.C. (1985). The Development of Computing in a Management School. *Management Education and Development*, 16(1), 54–65.

Horton, A. (2018, 11 April). Channelling 'The Social Network', Lawmaker Grills Zuckerberg on His Notorious Beginnings. *Washington Post*. https:// www .washingtonpost .com/ news/ the -switch/ wp/ 2018/ 04/ 11/ channeling -the -social -network-lawmaker-grills-zuckerberg-on-his-notorious-beginnings/

Hoskisson, R.E., Wan, W.P., Yiu, D., & Hitt, M.A. (1999). Theory and Research in Strategic Management: Swings of a pendulum. *Journal of Management*, 25(3), 417–456.

Huang, P., Wright, A.L., & Middleton, S. (2022). How Material Objects Shape Student Team Learning Processes. *Academy of Management Learning and Education*, 21(1), 35–60.

Huczynski, A. (1978). Unemployed Managers: A homogeneous group? *Management Education and Development*, 9(1), 21–25.

Huff, A.S. (2016). Unplugged – My own book review. *M@n@gement*, 19(3), 240–247.
Hughes, C. (2000). Painting New (Feminist) Pictures of Human Resource Development (and) Identifying Research Issues for Political Change. *Management Learning*, 31(1), 51–65.
Ireland, R.D., & Hitt, M.A. (1997). 'Strategy-as-Story': Clarifications and enhancements to Barry and Elmes' arguments. *Academy of Management Review*, 22(4), 840–852.
Jabali, M. (2021, 23 February). *A Corporate, Commodified Black History Month Is Taking Hold. We can't let it. The Guardian*. https:// www .theguardian .com/ commentisfree/ 2021/ feb/ 23/ a -corporate -commodified -Black -history -month -is -taking-hold-we-cant-let-it
Jackson, K.T. (2005). Breaking Down the Barriers: Bringing initiatives and reality into business ethics education. *Journal of Management Education*, 30(1), 65–89.
Jacobs, M. (1988). Don't Laugh – Socialism is popular. *New Socialist*, 56(Summer), 27–30.
James, W. (1922). *Pragmatism: A new name for some old ways of thinking*. Longmans, Green and Co.
Jarzabkowski, P., & Whittington, R. (2008a). A Strategy-As-Practice Approach to Strategy Research and Education. *Journal of Management Inquiry*. 17(4), 282–286.
Jarzabkowski, P., & Whittington, R. (2008b). Directions for a Troubled Discipline: Strategy research, teaching, and practice – introduction to the dialog. *Journal of Management Inquiry*, 17(4), 266–268.
Jelinek, M. (1986). In Search of Professional Ethics: Counterpoint. *Organizational Behavior Teaching Review*, 10(1), 50–55.
Jenster, P.V., & Duncan, D.D. (1987). Creating a Context of Commitment: Course agreements as a foundation. *Organizational Behavior Teaching Review*, 11(3), 60–71.
Johnson, R., & Blair, A. (1983). *Logical Self-Defence*. McGraw-Hill Ryerson.
Jones, C. (1994). A Contribution or a Commitment? Personal insights on diversity appreciation in the classroom. *Journal of Management Education*, 18(4), 432–437.
Jones, D.R., Visser, M., Stokes, P., Ortenblad, A., Deem, R., Rodgers, P., & Tarba, S.Y. (2020). The Performative University: 'Targets', 'terror', and 'taking back freedom' in academia. *Management Learning*, 51(4), 363–377.
Jones, T.M. (1989). Ethics Education in Business: Theoretical considerations. *Organizational Behavior Teaching Review*, 13(4), 1–18.
Joullie, J.E., & Spillane, R. (2020). *The Philosophical Foundations of Management Thought*. Lexington Books.
Kay, J. (2019). The Concept of the Corporation. *Business History*, 61(7), 1129–1143.
Keeley, M. (1983). Values in Organizational Theory and Management Education. *Academy of Management Review*, 8(3), 376–386.
Kerfoot, D., & Knights, D. (1993). Management, Masculinity and Manipulation: From paternalism to corporate strategy in financial services in Britain. *Journal of Management Studies*, 30(4), 659–678.
Kern, J.A. (2000). Manufacturing Power Relations: An organizational simulation. *Journal of Management Education*, 24(2), 254–275.
Kerr, R., & Robinson, S. (2012). From Symbolic Violence to Economic Violence: The globalizing of the Scottish banking elite. *Organization Studies*, 33(2), 247–266.
Kerr, S. (1975). On the Folly of Rewarding A while Hoping for B. *Academy of Management Journal*, 18(4), 769–783.

Khurana, R. (2007). *From Higher Aims to Hired Hands. The social transformation of American business schools and the unfulfilled promise of management as a profession.* Princeton University Press.

Kidwell, R.E., & Kochanowski, S.M. (2005). The Morality of Employee Theft: Teaching about ethics and deviant behavior in the workplace. *Journal of Management Education*, 29(1), 135–152.

King, A. (1993). From Sage on the Stage to Guide on the Side. *College Teaching*, 4(1), 30–35.

King, J.B. (1983). Teaching Business Ethics. *Exchange: The Organizational Behavior Teaching Journal*, 8(3), 25–32.

King, J.B. (1984). A Case for the Humanities Perspective. *Organizational Behavior Teaching Review*, 9(1), 13–30.

Kingsnorth, P. (2018). Introduction. In W. Berry (ed.), *The World Ending Fire. The essential Wendell Berry* (pp. iii–vii). Penguin Press.

Kline, M. (1999). Narrating the Grotesque: The rhetoric of humor in John Kennedy Toole's *A Confederacy of Dunces*. *Southern Quarterly*, 37(3), 283–291.

Knights, D., Huber, G., & Longman, R. (2022). Critical Management Education: Selected auto-ethnographic vignettes on how attachment to identity may disrupt learning. *Management Learning*, 53(3), 605–616.

Kogut, M., Thaning, M.S., & Birkstead, N. (2021). Intellectual Emancipation and Minimal Humanism – The relevance of Jacques Rancière in business school teaching. *Management Learning*, 52(2), 165–187.

Kuechler, W., & Stedham, Y. (2018). Management Education and Transformational Learning: The integration of mindfulness in an MBA Course. *Journal of Management Education*, 42(1), 8–33.

Laasch, O., Lindebaum, D., & Caza, A. (2022a). Constructing Ontological Foundations for Management Learning and Education Research. *Academy of Management Learning and Education*, 21(4), 525–531.

Larson, G. (2023). *The Far Side.* https://www.thefarside.com/

Lawson, T. (2019). *The Nature of Social Reality: Issues in social ontology.* Routledge.

Learmonth, M. (2007). Critical Management Education in Action: Personal tales of management unlearning. *Academy of Management Learning and Education*, 6(1), 109–113.

Lefevre, D., & Caporarello, L. (2022). Management Education and Digital Technology: Choices for strategy and innovation. In M.R. Fellenz, S. Hoidn, & M. Brady (eds), *The Future of Management Education* (pp. 153–171). Routledge.

Leigh, J.S.A., & Rivers, C. (2023). Reflect, Rethink, and Redesign: Responses to privilege in management education. *Journal of Management Education*, 47(1), 3–10.

Lessam, S. (1974). Self, Management and Society: Some implications for management education. *Management Education and Development*, 5(1), 17–34.

LeVan, S. (1987). 'A Community of Writers': Collaborative writing for the organization. *Organizational Behavior Teaching Review*, 11(3), 127–130.

Levinson, H. (1965). Reciprocation: The relationship between man and organization. *Administrative Science Quarterly*, 9(4), 370–390.

Lewicki, R. (1975). The Research-Teaching Bind: Increasing conflict in the 1980s. *The Teaching of Organizational Behavior*, 1(4), 20–24.

Lewicki, R. (2002). From the Editor. *Academy of Management Learning and Education*, 1(1), 8–12.

Lewis, C.S. (1975). *The Abolition of Man: Or reflections on education with special reference to the teaching of English in the upper forms of schools.* Macmillan.

Lim, A., Qing, J., Chen, D., & Eyring, A.R. (2014). Netting the Evidence: A review of on-line evidence-based management resources. *Academy of Management Learning and Education,* 13(3), 495–503.

Lindebaum, D. (2023). Management Learning and Education as 'Big Picture' Social Science. *Academy of Management Learning and Education.*

Linowes, R.G. (1992). Filling a Gap in Management Education: Giving leadership talks in the classroom. *Journal of Management Education,* 16(1), 6–24.

Lips-Wiersma, M., & Morris, L. (2017). *The Map of Meaning.* Routledge.

Liu, H. (2022). How We Learn Whiteness: Disciplining and resisting management knowledge. *Management Learning,* 53(5), 776–796.

Lo, K.D. (2023). Contextual and Experiential Understandings of Privilege as Intersectional. *Journal of Management Education,* 47(1), 79–103.

Lorbiecki, A. (2001). Changing Views on Diversity Management: The rise of the learning perspective and the need to recognize social and political contradictions. *Management Learning,* 32(3), 345–361.

Lucas, G. (Director). (1977). *Star Wars.* [Film]. 20th Century-Fox.

Macalpine, M., & Marsh, S. (2005). 'On Being White: There's nothing I can say': Exploring whiteness and power in organizations. *Management Learning,* 36(4), 429–450.

MacIntyre, A.D. (1981). *After Virtue.* University of Notre Dame Press.

MacIntyre, A.D. (1995). The Brent Spar Incident – A milestone event. *Marine Pollution Bulletin,* 30(9), 578.

Maclagan, P. (1991). 'Having and Being' in Organisations. *Management Education and Development,* 22(3), 234–241.

Malekzadeh, A.R. (1998). Diversity, Integration, Globalization, and Critical Thinking in the Upper Division. *Journal of Management Education,* 22(5), 590–603.

Maloni, M.J., Smith, S.D., & Napshin, S. (2012). A Methodology for Building Faculty Support for the United Nations Principles for Responsible Management Education. *Journal of Management Education,* 36(3), 312–336.

Marable, M. (2015). *How Capitalism Underdeveloped Black America: Problems in race, political economy, and society.* Haymarket Books.

Marcuse, H. (1964). *One-Dimensional Man: Studies in the ideology of advanced industrial society.* Beacon Press.

Marcuse, H. (1968). *Negations: Essays in critical theory.* Penguin.

Marshall, L.C. (1921). *Business Administration.* University of Chicago Press.

Marshall, S.J. (2018). Technology as a Catalyst for Change. In S.J. Marshall (ed.), *Shaping the University of the Future: Using technology to catalyse change in university learning and teaching* (pp. 147–166). Springer.

Martin, R. (1977). *The Sociology of Power.* Routledge and Kegan Paul.

Mathieu, C. (2009). Practising Gender in Organizations: The critical gap between practical and discursive consciousness. *Management Learning,* 40(2), 177–193.

McCann, L., Granter, E., Hyde, P., & Aroles, J. (2020). Upon the Gears and Upon the Wheels: Terror convergence and total administration in the neoliberal university. *Management Learning,* 51(4), 431–451.

McCormick, D.W., & Fleming, J. (1990). Teaching Ethics Means Practicing Ethics: When a student says his company is breaking the law. *Organizational Behavior Teaching Review,* 14(3), 14–22.

McDermid, C.D. (1960). How Money Motivates Men. *Business Horizons,* 3(4), 93–100.

McDonald, J. (2013). Coming Out in the Field: A queer reflexive account of shifting researcher identity. *Management Learning*, 44(2), 127–143.

McDonald, J. (2016). Expanding Queer Reflexivity: The closet as a guiding metaphor for reflexive practice. *Management Learning*, 47(4), 391–406.

McFarland, D.E. (1959). Education for Management: New directions and new challenges. *The Journal of the Academy of Management*, 2(1), 39–46.

McLaren, P.G. (2019). Stop Blaming Gordon and Howell: Unpacking the complex history behind the research-based model of education. *Academy of Management Learning and Education*, 18(1), 43–58.

McLaren, P.G., Bridgman, T., Cummings, S., Lubinski, C., O'Connor, E., Spender, J-C., & Durepos, G. (2021). New Times, New Histories of the Business School. *Academy of Management Learning and Education*, 20(3), 293–299.

McQuarrie, F.A.E. (1998). Expanding the Concept of Diversity: Discussing sexual orientation in the management classroom. *Journal of Management Education*, 22(2), 162–172.

Messerly, J. (2015). *Summary of John Rawls' Moral Theory*. Reason and Meaning. https://reasonandmeaning.com/2015/04/13/john-rawls-moral-contractarianism/

Mezoff, B. (1983). Managing a Diverse Workforce: Teaching MBAs about gay/lesbian issues in management. *Exchange: The Organizational Behavior Teaching Journal*, 8(1), 31–33.

Middleton, S. (2022). For You? Using TikTok to teach key content. *Management Teaching Review*, 7(3), 226–235.

Middleton, S. (2009). Reputation Management in the Salvation Army: A narrative study. *Journal of Management Inquiry*, 18(2), 145–157.

Middleton, S., & Alday, S. (2023). Guest Editorial: Learning To Not Teach. *Journal of Management Education* 47(6), 566–571.

Miesing, P. (1998). B-Schools on the I-Way: Avoiding potholes, dead ends, and crashes. *Journal of Management Education*, 22(6), 735–770.

Milbank, J., & Pabst, A. (2016). *The Politics of Virtue: Post-liberalism and the human future*. Rowman & Littlefield International.

Miller, J.A. (1991). Experiencing Management: A comprehensive, 'hands-on' model for the introductory undergraduate management course. *Journal of Management Education*, 15(2), 151–169.

Mingers, J. (2000). What Is It to Be Critical? Teaching a critical approach to management undergraduates. *Management Learning*, 31(2), 219–237.

Mintzberg, H. (1975). The Manager's Job: Folklore and fact. *Harvard Business Review*, 53(4), 49–61.

Mintzberg, H. (1987). Crafting Strategy. *Harvard Business Review*, 65, 66–75.

Mintzberg, H. (2004). *Managers, Not MBAs: A hard look at the soft practice of managing and management development*. Berrett-Koehler.

Mir, A. (2003). The Hegemonic Discourse of Management Texts. *Journal of Management Education*, 27(6), 734–738.

Mizejewski, L., Zuk, T.D., Feil, K., Fogel, J.M., Hoffner, C.A., & Jackson, M.M. (2021). *Our Blessed Rebel Queen: Essays on Carrie Fisher and Princess Leia*. Wayne State University Press.

Mobasser, N. (1987). Marx and Self-Realisation. *New Left Review*, 161(Jan/Feb), 119–128.

Moergen, K.J.N., & Kish-Gephart, J.J. (2023). Bringing 'Class' Into the Classroom: Addressing social class privilege through management education. *Journal of Management Education*, 47(1), 11–39.

Moon, C. (1989). Green Bills or Pound Coins – Can business ethics resolve the dilemma? *Management Education and Development*, 20(3), 143–152.

Moore, L.F., Shetzer, L., & Stackman, R.W. (1992). Frond Lake: An environmental policy role play. *Journal of Management Education*, 16(2), 146–162.

Moreau, J. (2021, 4 August). *From 'Kiss of Death' to Competitive Edge: Out athletes finally score big endorsements*. NBC News. https://www.nbcnews.com/nbc-out/out-news/kiss-death-competitive-edge-athletes-finally-score-big-endorsements-rcna1586

Moser, C., Den Hond, F., & Lindebaum, D. (2022). Morality in the Age of Artificially Intelligent Algorithms. *Academy of Management Learning and Education*, 21(1), 139–155.

Mowday, R.T. (2006). If Special Issues of Journals Are Not So Special, Why Has Their Use Proliferated? *Journal of Management Inquiry*, 15(4), 389–393.

Neal, M., & Finlay, J.L. (2008). American Hegemony and Business Education in the Arab World. *Journal of Management Education*, 32(1), 38–83.

New Revised Standard Version Bible (2023). The National Council of Churches.

Nisbet, E., & Fowler, C. (1995). Is Metal Disposal Toxic to Deep Oceans? *Nature*, 375(6534), 715.

Nixon, B. (1986). Power and Patterns in People and Organisations. *Management Education and Development*, 17(4), 336–344.

Nordback, E., Hakonen, M., & Tienari, J. (2022). Academic Identities and Sense of Place: A collaborative autoethnography in the neoliberal university. *Management Learning*, 53(2), 331–349.

Nyad, D. (2016, 17 April). *Transgender Athletes Raise Questions for Future Olympic Games*. NPR. https://www.npr.org/2016/08/17/490314013/transgender-athletes-raise-questions-for-future-olympic-games

Owen, D. (1983). The Acceptance of Authority: A case study. *Management Education and Development*, 14(2), 113–117.

Ozcelik, H., & Paprika, Z.Z. (2010). Developing Emotional Awareness in Cross-Cultural Communication: A videoconferencing approach. *Journal of Management Education*, 34(5), 671–699.

Pabst, A. (2019). *The Demons of Liberal Democracy*. Wiley.

Parker, M. (2002). *Against Management: Organization in the age of managerialism*. Polity Press.

Parker, M. (2018a). *Shut Down the Business School: What's wrong with management education*. Pluto Press.

Parker, M. (2018b, 27 April). Why We Should Bulldoze the Business School. *The Guardian*. https://www.theguardian.com/news/2018/apr/27/bulldoze-the-business-school

Parsley, S. (2022). Feeling Your Way as an Occupational Minority: The gendered sensilisation of women electronic music artists. *Management Learning*, 53(4), 697–717.

Paton, S., Chia, R., & Burt, G. (2014). Relevance or 'Relevate'? How university business schools can add value through reflexively learning from strategic partnerships with business. *Management Learning*, 45(3), 267–288.

Payne, S.L. (1993). Ethics Integration: The management/organizational behavior fundamentals course and broader concerns. *Journal of Management Education*, 17(4), 472–484.

Pedler, M. (1981). Men and Management. *Management Education and Development*, 12(1), 15–18.

Peirce, C. (1878). How to Make Our Ideas Clear. *Popular Science Monthly*, 12 (January), 286–302.

Peirce, C. (1901). Truth and Falsity and Error. In C. Hartshorne & P. Weiss (eds), *Collected Papers of Charles Sanders Peirce*, vols V and VI (pp. 394–398). Harvard University Press.

Peirce, C. (2016). How to Make Our Ideas Clear. *Revisita Filosofia UIS*, 15(2), 287–303.

Peoples, R. (2009). Preparing Today for a Sustainable Future. *Journal of Management Education*, 33(3), 376–383.

Perrin, N. (1974). *The New Testament: An introduction*. Harcourt Brace Jovanovich.

Peters, T.J., & Waterman, R.H. (1982). *In Search of Excellence: Lessons from America's best-run companies*. Profile Business.

Peterson, C.H., Rice, S.D., Short, J.W., Esler, D., Bodkin, J.L., Ballachey, B.E., & Irons, D.B. (2003). Long-Term Ecosystem Response to the Exxon Valdez Oil Spill. *Science*, 302(5653), 2082–2086.

Pfeffer, J., & Fong, C.T. (2004). The Business School 'Business': Some lessons from the US experience. *Journal of Management Studies*, 41(8), 1501–1520.

Pheysey, D. (1980). Book Reviews: *Control and Ideology in Organizations*. *Management Education and Development*, 11(3), 224–225.

Pielstick, C.D. (2005). Teaching Spiritual Synchronicity in a Business Leadership Class. *Journal of Management Education*, 29(1), 153–168.

Pierson, F.C. (1959). *The Education of American Businessmen*. McGraw-Hill.

Pina e Cunha, M., Giustiniano, L., Rego, A., & Clegg, S. (2017). Mission Impossible? The paradoxes of stretch goal setting. *Management Learning*, 48(2), 140–157.

Pio, E., & Syed, J. (2020). Stelae from Ancient India: Pondering anew through historical empathy for diversity. *Management Learning*, 51(1), 109–129.

Porter, L.W. (1983). Teaching Managerial Competencies: An overview. *Exchange: The Organizational Behavior Teaching Society*, 8(2), 8–9.

Porter, L.W., & McKibben, L.E. (1988). *Management Education and Development: Drift or thrust into the 21st century*. McGraw-Hill.

Porter, M. (1979). How Competitive Forces Shape Strategy. *Harvard Business Review*, 57, 137–145.

Powell, G.N., & Taylor, K.B. (1998). Beyond O.J.: Examining race relations in the workplace. *Journal of Management Education*, 22(2), 208–217.

Power, D.J., Roth, R.M., & Aldag, R.J. (1993). A Review of Decision-Aiding Software: A management education perspective. *Journal of Management Education*, 17(4), 520–529.

Powers, J. (1975). The Blind Decision-Makers: The role of non-verbal communication. *The Teaching of Organizational Behavior*, 1(1), 1–35.

Priem, R.L. (2006). What Happens When Special Issues Just Aren't 'Special' Anymore? *Journal of Management Inquiry*, 15(4), 383–388.

Prieto, L., Phipps, S., Stott, N., & Giugni, L. (2021). Teaching Cooperative Business: The 'Bluefield Experiment' and the future of Black business schools. *Academy of Management Learning and Education*, 20(3), 320–341.

Pugh, D. (1970). Foreword. *Management Education and Development*, 1(1), 1–2.

Pym, D. (1990). Post-Paradigm Inquiry. In J. Hassard & D. Pym (eds), *The Theory and Philosophy of Organizations: Critical issues and new perspectives* (pp. 233–241). Routledge.

Rabinowitz, S., & Fender, C.M. (2018). Seeing Is Believing – But is it accurate? Eyewitness lessons from 12 Angry Men. *Management Teaching Review*, 5(4), 302–310.

Ramsey, V.J., & Fitzgibbons, D.E. (2005). Being in the Classroom. *Journal of Management Education*, 29(2), 333–356.

Randolph, W.A., Ferrie, J., & Palmer, D.D. (1976). A Simulation for Developing Od Intervention Skills. *The Teaching of Organizational Behavior*, 2(3), 31–33.

Ratle, O., Robinson, S., Bristow, A., & Kerr, R. (2020). Mechanisms of Micro-Terror? Early career CMS academics' experiences of 'targets and terror' in contemporary business schools. *Management Learning*, 51(4), 452–471.

Rawls, J. (1971). *A Theory of Justice*. Harvard University Press.

Readings, B. (1996). *The University in Ruins*. Harvard University Press.

Ready, R.K. (1975). Management Education: An agenda for 1985. *The Teaching of Organizational Behavior*, 1(4), 14–19.

Reardon, K.A. (2016). Using the Qualitative Interview in the Classroom to Help Students Make Connections Among Course Content, Social Capital, and Careers. *Management Teaching Review*, 1(1), 26–33.

Redlich, F. (1957). Academic Education for Business: Its development and the contribution of Ingnaz Jastrow (1856–1937) in commemoration of the hundredth anniversary of Jastrow's birth. *The Business History Review*, 31(1), 35–91.

Rhee, J. (2018). *The Robotic Imaginary. The human and the price of dehumanized labor*. University of Minnesota Press.

Rhee, K.S. (2003). Self-Directed Learning: To be aware or not to be aware. *Journal of Management Education*, 27(5), 568–589.

Ringer, F. (1990). The Intellectual Field, Intellectual History, and the Sociology of Knowledge. *Theory and Society*, 19(3), 269–294.

Rivers, C., & Holland, A. (2022). Management Education and Artificial Intelligence: Toward personalized learning. In M.R. Fellenz, S. Hoidn, & M. Brady (eds), *The Future of Management Education* (pp. 184–204). Routledge.

Roberts, C. (2008). Developing Future Leaders: The role of reflection in the classroom. *Journal of Leadership Education*, 7(1), 116–130.

Rogers, J.C., Williams, T.G., & McLeod Jr, R. (1988). Microcomputer Usage in Marketing Departments of Fortune 500 Firms: What should marketing students study? *Organizational Behavior Teaching Review*, 12(1), 18–23.

Rokeach, M. (1968). *Beliefs, Attitudes, and Values*. Jossey-Bass.

Ronan, N.J. (1993). Developing the African Manager – The good, the bad, and the competent. *Management Education and Development*, 24(4), 388–394.

Rosenthal, C. (2021). Reckoning with Slavery: How revisiting management's uncomfortable past can help us confront challenges today. *Academy of Management Learning and Education*, 20(3), 467–472.

Rosile, G.A., & Boje, D.M. (1996). Pedagogy for the Postmodern Management Classroom: Greenback company. In D.M. Boje, J. Tojo, & R.P. Gephart (eds), *Postmodern Management and Organization Theory* (pp. 225–250). Sage Publications.

Rudin, J., Yang, Y., Ruane, S., Ross, L., Farro, A., & Billing, T. (2016). Transforming Attitudes About Transgender Employee Rights. *Journal of Management Education*, 40(1), 30–46.

Rumens, N. (2017). Queering Lesbian, Gay, Bisexual and Transgender Identities in Human Resource Development and Management Education Contexts. *Management Learning*, 48(2), 227–242.

Rutledge, F. (2015). *The Crucifixion: Understanding the death of Jesus Christ*. Wm. B. Eerdmans Publishing Company.

Ryazanova, O., Wright, A.L., & Laasch, O. (2021). Studying the Ongoing Change at the Individual Level: Who am I (becoming) as a management educator and researcher? *Academy of Management Learning and Education*, 20(4), 497–500.

Saad, L. (2020). *Me and White Supremacy: Combat racism, change the world, and become a good ancestor*. Sourcebooks.

Salaman, G., & Thompson, K. (eds) (1980). *Control and Ideology in Organizations*. The Open University Press.

Sales, N.J. (2016) *American Girls: Social media and the secret lives of teenagers*. Alfred A Knopf.

Schmidt, G.B. (2016). Using Pinterest in the Management Classroom. *Management Teaching Review*, 1(2), 79–84.

Schor, S.M., Sims, R.R., & Dennehy, R.F. (1996). Power and Diversity: Sensitizing yourself and others through self-reflection and storytelling. *Journal of Management Education*, 20(2), 242–257.

Schultheiss, E.E. (1990). Practicing Ethics: A corporate training response. *Organizational Behavior Teaching Review*, 14(3), 27–31.

Schwabenland, C. (2011). Surprise and Awe: Learning from Indigenous managers and implications for management education. *Journal of Management Education*, 35(1), 138–153.

Schwarz, J.L., & Murphy, T.E. (2008). Human Capital Metrics: An approach to teaching using data and metrics to design and evaluate management practices. *Journal of Management Education*, 32(2), 164–182.

Scott, D.J.R. (1970). All Economists, All Politicians, All Finders-Out. *Management Education and Development*, 1(1), 60–64.

Scott, D.J.R. (1972). Creative Management Mondays 9:30 am: The arts side of business education. *Management Education and Development*, 3(2), 113–124.

Seashore, E.W. (1976). The New Role for White Male Managers. *The Teaching of Organizational Behavior*, 2(1), 43–45.

Selznick, P. (1957). *Leadership in Administration*. Row, Peterson.

Shah, U., O'Reilly, D., & Analoui, B. (2022). Who Is Responsible for Responsible Business Education? Insights into the dialectical interrelations of dimensions of responsibility. *Management Learning* 54(4).

Shannin, T. (1988). Introduction to Aganbegyan. *New Left Review*, 169(May/June), 88–88.

Shipley, P. (2019, 20 November). *Professor Denis Pym*. Birkbeck University of London. https://www.bbk.ac.uk/about-us/obituaries/professor-denis-pym

Shivarajan, S., & Andrews, R. (2021). Using Improvisation to Develop Emotional Intelligence. *Management Teaching Review*, 6(2), 152–163.

Siegall, M. (1988). The Simplistic Five: An integrative framework for teaching motivation. *Organizational Behavior Teaching Review*, 12(4), 141–143.

Sikula, A. (1995). Diversity: A good idea or bad idea? *Journal of Management Education*, 19(2), 254–262.

Simha, A., Armstrong, J.P., & Albert, J.F. (2012). Attitudes and Behaviors of Academic Dishonesty and Cheating: Do ethics education and ethics training affect either attitudes or behaviors? *Journal of Business Education*, 9, 129–144.

Simpson, R. (2006). Masculinity and Management Education: Feminizing the MBA. *Academy of Management Learning and Education*, 5(2), 182–193.

Sims, R.R., & Brinkmann, J. (2003). Enron Ethics (Or: Culture matters more than codes). *Journal of Business Ethics*, 45, 243–256.

Sinclair, A. (2000). Teaching Managers About Masculinities: Are you kidding? *Management Learning*, 31(1), 83–101.

Sine, R. (2011, 4 November). *The World's Richest and Fittest Guys*. Men's Health. https://www.menshealth.com/trending-news/a19540258/worlds-fittest-richest-guys/

Siu, R.G.H. (1979). *The Craft of Power*. John Wiley & Sons.

Smircich, L., & Stubbart, C. (1985). Strategic Management in an Enacted World. *Academy of Management Review*, 10(4), 724–736.

Smith, D., Hart, D., & McCloskey, J. (1994). Greening the Business School: Environmental education and the business curriculum. *Management Learning*, 25(3), 475–488.

Snell, R. (1986). Questioning the Ethics of Management Development: A critical review. *Management Education and Development*, 17(1), 43–64.

Snell, R. (1989). Applying Socialist Ethics to Management Development. *Management Education and Development*, 20(3), 153–167.

Solomon, G.T. (1979). A Computer Simulation Exercise to Acquire Interpersonal Competence. *Exchange: The Organizational Behavior Teaching Journal*, 4(2), 35.

Spark, M. (1961). *The Prime of Miss Jean Brodie*. Macmillan.

Sparks, W.L. (2017). My 'F' in Life: A tribute to Jerry B. Harvey. *Journal of Management, Spirituality & Religion*, 14(2), 117–123.

Sparks, W.L. (forthcoming). *Actualized Teamwork: Managing the shadow side of group culture*. Society for Human Resource Management Press.

Spelman, D., Crary, M., Weathersby, R., & Bocialetti, G. (1986). Men Students in 'Women in Management' Courses: Learning and dilemmas. *Organizational Behavior Teaching Review*, 10(4), 89–97.

Spencer, N. (Host) (2021, 13 July). What Comes After Liberalism? In conversation with Adrian Pabst. [Audio podcast episode] In *Reading Our Times*. Theos Think Tank. https://readingourtimes.podigee.io/17-adrianpabst

Spicer, A. (2005). Conferences. In C. Jones & D. O'Doherty (eds), *Organize! Manifestos for the Business School of Tomorrow* (pp. 21–27). Davlin.

Spillane, R., & Joullie, J.E. (2021). The Decline of Authority and the Rise of Managerialism. *Organization*, 30(5).

Sports Business Journal (2021, 2 June). Adidas Putting More Money, Effort into Growing WNBA Roster. *Sports Business Journal*. https://www.sportsbusinessjournal .com/Daily/Issues/2021/06/02/Marketing-and-Sponsorship/Adidas-WNBA.aspx

Sprung, S. (2022, 29 November). *Carl Nassib & Rayze: Connecting non-profits for greater good*. Boardroom. https://boardroom.tv/carl-nassib-rayze/

Sroufe, R., Sivasubramaniam, N., Ramos, D., & Saiia, D. (2015). Aligning the PRME: How study abroad nurtures responsible leadership. *Journal of Management Education*, 39(2), 244–275.

Star Wars Ventures (1977). Interview with George Lucas. *Star Wars Souvenir Program*. Star Wars Ventures.

Stark, J.B. (2019). Where Did All the People Go? The view from the Dean's office at 30,000 feet. *Journal of Management Education*, 43(3), 304–310.

Starr-Glass, D. (2004). Exploring Organisational Culture: Teaching notes on metaphor, totem, and archetypal images. *Journal of Management Education*, 28(3), 356–371.

Stavrou, E.T. (2017). The Work of Jerry Harvey on Student Cheating. *Journal of Management, Spirituality & Religion*, 14(2), 124–130.

Strauss, G. (1977). Sex and Minority Leadership Roles in an Experiential Learning Class. *The Teaching of Organizational Behavior*, 2(4), 30–32.

Summers, D.J., Boje, D.M., Dennehy, R.F., & Rosile, G.A. (1997). Deconstructing the Organizational Behavior Text. *Journal of Management Education*, 21(3), 343–360.

Swierca, P.M., & Ross, K.T. (2003). Rational, Human, Political, and Symbolic Text in Harvard Business School Cases: A study of structure and content. *Journal of Management Education*, 27(4), 407–430.

Talpaert, R. (1978). Management in Modern Society: A pro-active approach. *Management Education and Development*, 9(3), 139–150.

Tangihaere, T.M., & Twiname, L. (2011). Providing Space for Indigenous Knowledge. *Journal of Management Education*, 35(1), 102–118.

Taylor, S. (2018). Forming Character in Business School Leadership Education: Rejoinder to 'the development of leader character through crucible moments'. *Journal of Management Education*, 42(2), 301–305.

Taylor, S.S., & Statler, M. (2014). Material Matters: Increasing emotional engagement in learning. *Journal of Management Education*, 38(4), 586–607.

Taylor, V.B. (2018). Afraid of the Deep: Reflections and analysis of a role-play exercise gone wrong. *Journal of Management Education*, 42(6), 772–782.

Tikkanen, H. (2023). Towards Americanisation and the Corporate University in an Elite Business School: A leadership history of the Helsinki School of Economics/ Aalto University School of Business, 1974–2022. *Business History*, 1–23.

Tolstoy, L. (1993). *War and Peace*. Translated by L. Maude & A. Maude. Wordsworth.

Toole, J.K. (1980). *A Confederacy of Dunces*. LSU Press.

Tosey, P. (1989). Politics in Context: Our secret lives. *Management Education and Development*, 20(3), 254–269.

Toubiana, M. (2012). Business Pedagogy for Social Justice? An exploratory investigation of business faculty perspectives of social justice in business education. *Management Learning*, 45(1), 81–102.

Treadwell, T.W., Leach, E.A., Kellar, H., Lewis, R., & Mittan, B. (1998). Collaborative Teaching Over the Internet. *Journal of Management Education*, 22(4), 498–508.

Twain, M. (2010). *The Adventures of Huckelberry Finn*. William Collins.

United Nations (2007). *Global Compact: The Principles of Responsible Management Education*. https://www.unprme.org/

Vaill, P.B. (1979). Cookbooks, Auctions, and Claptrap Cocoons: A commentary on the field of organizational behavior. *Exchange: The Organizational Behavior Teaching Journal*, 4(1), 3–6.

Vaill, P.B. (1981). Exploration and Discovery: Or how can you tell whether you're getting anywhere when you don't know where you're going? *Exchange: The Organizational Behavior Teaching Journal*, 6(2), 15–19.

Vaill, P.B. (1984). Commentary on Terry Connolly's 'Choice' Metaphor. *Organizational Behavior Teaching Review*, 9(1), 11–12.

Vaill, P.B. (1996). *Learning as a Way of Being: Strategies for survival in a world of permanent white water*. Jossey-Bass.

Vaill, P.B. (1997). Meditations on a Poet's Overalls. In R. Andre & P.J. Frost (eds), *Researchers Hooked on Teaching: Noted scholars discuss the synergies of teaching and research* (pp. 258–280). Sage.

Valliant, G. (1977). *Adaptation to Life*. Little, Brown and Company.

Van Buren, H.J. III, & Hood, J.N. (2010). Building Student Competency to Develop Power and Influence Through Social Capital. *Journal of Management Education*, 35(5), 648–678.

Van Buskirk, W., & London, M. (2008). Inviting the Muse into the Classroom: Poetic license in management education. *Journal of Management Education*, 32(3), 294–315.

Van Buskirk, W., & London, M. (2012). Poetry as Deep Intelligence: A qualitative approach for the organizational behavior classroom. *Journal of Management Education*, 36(5), 636–668.

Varian, H.R. (2010). Computer Mediated Transactions. *American Economic Review*, 100(2), 1–10.

Varma, R., & Varma, D.R. (2005). The Bhopal Disaster of 1984. *Bulletin of Science, Technology, & Society*, 25(1), 37–45.

Veiga, J.F. (1978). An Instrument for Mirroring Personal Leadership Behavior: The leadership style inventory. *Exchange: The Organizational Behavior Teaching Journal*, 3(2), 34.

Verbos, A.K., Kennedy, D.M., & Gladstone, J.S. (2011). 'Coyote Was Walking …': Management education in Indian time. *Journal of Management Education*, 35(1), 51–65.

Vince, R. (1990). Management by Avoidance: Male power in local government. *Management Education and Development*, 22(1), 50–59.

Viswanathan, M. (2012). Curricular Innovations on Sustainability and Subsistence Marketplaces: Philosophical, substantive, and methodological orientations. *Journal of Management Education*, 36(3), 389–427.

Voltaire. (1759). *Candide: Or, all for the best*. Cramer.

Wachowskis, The (Directors). (1999). *The Matrix*. [Film]. Warner Brothers, Village Roadshow Pictures, Groucho Il Film Partnership, Silver Pictures.

Wall Street Journal (1995, 10 October). Simpson Verdict Is Seen as a Milestone for Workplace Relations. *Wall Street Journal*, A1.

Wallo, A., Martin, J., Sparrhoff, G., & Kock, H. (2022). Balancing 'Critique for Improvement' With 'Critique for Emancipation' in Management Learning and Education. *Journal of Management Education*, 46(3), 506–530.

Wanderley, S., Alcadipan, R., & Barros, A. (2021). Recentering the Global South in the Making of Business School Histories: Dependency ambiguity in action. *Academy of Management Learning and Education*, 20(3), 361–381.

Waters, H. (1989). Making the Organizational Behavior Course Relevant to Black Students. *Organizational Behavior Teaching Review*, 13(3), 38–44.

Watkin, C., & Keller, T. (2022). *Biblical Critical Theory: How the Bible's unfolding story makes sense of modern life and culture*. Harper Collins Christian Publishing.

Weber, M. (1968). *Economy and Society: An outline of interpretive sociology*. Bedminster Press.

Wharton, J. (1875). *National Self-Protection*. The American Iron and Steel Association.

Wheelwright, S.C. (1972). Introducing Managers to Management Science and Computers Through Modelling and Simulation. *Management Education and Development*, 2(3), 149–157.

White, J., & Taft, S. (2004). Frameworks for Teaching and Learning Business Ethics Within the Global Context: Background of ethical theories. *Journal of Management Education*, 28(4), 407–518.

Whitley, R.D. (1977). Book Reviews: *The Sociology of Power*: Roderick Martin. *Management Education and Development*, 8(3), 155–156.

Whittington, R., Jarzabkowski, P., Mayer, M., Mounoud, E., Nahapiet, J., & Rouleau, L. (2003). Taking Strategy Seriously: Responsibility and reform for an important social practice. *Journal of Management Inquiry*, 12(4), 396–409.

Wickens, J. (1979). Book Reviews: *The Craft of Power* R.G.H. Siu. *Management Education and Development*, 10(3), 222–223.

Williams, R. (2023, 5 March). Interview With a (Reformed) Vampire. *The Sunday Times*, 18–26.

Willmott, H. (1994). Management Education: Provocations to a debate. *Management Learning*, 25(1), 105–136.

Willmott, H. (2012). Critical Management Learning. In J. Burgoyne & M. Reynolds (eds), *Management Learning: Integrating perspectives in theory and practice* (pp. 161–174). Sage Publications.

Woods, C., Dell, K., & Carroll, B., (2022). Decolonizing the Business School: Reconstructing the entrepreneurship classroom through indigenizing pedagogy and learning. *Academy of Management Learning and Education*, 21(1), 82–100.

Wright, A.L., Irving, G., Hibbert, P., & Greenfield, G., (2018). Student Understandings of Evidence-Based Management: Ways of doing and being. *Academy of Management Learning and Education*, 17(4), 453–473.

Wright, R.E. (2010). Teaching History in Business Schools: An insider's view. *Academy of Management Learning and Education*, 9(4), 697–700.

Yates, J.E., & Summers, M. (1986). In Search of Professional Ethics. *Organizational Behavior Teaching Review*, 10(1), 35–49.

Young-Ferris, A., & Voola, R. (2023). Disrupting Privilege as Power and Control: Re-imagining business and the appreciation of Indigenous stewardship in management education curricula. *Journal of Management Education*, 47(1), 135–153.

Zawadzki, M., & Jensen, T. (2020). Bullying and the Neoliberal University: A co-authored ethnography. *Management Learning*, 51(4), 398–413.

Zidulka, A., & Kajzer Mitchell, I. (2018). Creativity or Cooptation? Thinking beyond instrumentalism when teaching design thinking. *Journal of Management Education*, 42(6), 749–760.

Zoogah, B.D. (2021). Historicizing Management and Organization in Africa. *Academy of Management Learning and Education*, 20(3), 382–406.

Zuboff, S. (2019). *The Age of Surveillance Capitalism: The fight for a human future at the new frontier of power*. Profile.

Zuboff, S., Moellers, N., Murakami Wood, D., & Lyon, D. (2019). Surveillance Capitalism: An interview with Shoshanna Zuboff. *Surveillance and Society*, 17(1/2), 257–266.

Index